# Mesilla Comes Alive

# *Mesilla Comes Alive: A History of Mesilla and its Valley*

by
C.W. "Buddy" Ritter
with
Craig Holden

Ritter Publications

For futher information, please address:
Ritter Publications
P.O. Box 905
Las Cruces, NM 88004

Book designed and typeset by Michael Biddle

Cover art: "Old Mesilla Plaza," by Leon Trousset, circa
1885-1886,
used by permission, courtesy of the National Portrait
Gallery.

ISBN: 978-0-9908783-0-8

# Dedication

To Dr. Edwin Burt, M.D., my great-great-grandfather, and
Supreme Court Justice Richmond Palmer Barnes, my great-grandfather,
who founded our Mesilla Valley Family.

And to Winfield Fulton Ritter, my grandfather
and John Barnes Ritter, my father,
who both had such a significant influence upon my life.

# Table of Contents

# List of Illustrations

# Preface

Our family stories from the past seven generations really spurred my original interest in the history of Mesilla and the Mesilla Valley. It is now more than 20 years ago since I first began thinking of a project to somehow capture that history. The six years that I served as President of the Board of Regents of the Museums of New Mexico was an important period because I was able to spend time in the State Archives accumulating boxes of information, photographs and maps.

Later, I put together a detailed slide show that began to illustrate and illuminate this history. It was met with great enthusiasm by many people, and their encouragement kept me going and led ultimately to this project.

But being a hotelier, restaurateur and banker, I had difficulty finding time to work on the book. I finally decided, "Now is the time. I must get started." Soon after making that decision, I realized that I needed help.

A year ago I met Craig Holden, local novelist and professor at New Mexico State University. When we met and began talking, I realized that he shared my vision of what this book could be, and we began to work together to make it happen. I am very pleased now to present to you the result of that work -- *Mesilla Comes Alive: A History of Mesilla and Its Valley.*

Local historians have already said that it is an excellent book and will be regarded as part of the historical canon on the history of Mesilla and the Mesilla Valley. One thing the book seeks to do is to dispel some of the common myths regarding the area, such as that Las Cruces was named for crosses in a makeshift cemetery when it was really named for being a crossroads. It also points out a number of little known facts or insights, such as the notion that when Mesilla was named by Onate, it would become the oldest permanent place name in New Mexico, some nine years before Santa Fe was named.

There are many more interesting insights and revelations here, some of which challenge previous thinking. There is also a new translation of a little-seen document written by Albert Fountain in the early 1880s. I trust that, if you share my fascination with and love of this area, you will enjoy reading this book as much as I enjoyed putting it together.

# Part I

## The Spaniards in New Mexico

# Before

People have lived in the Mesilla Valley, on and off, for a very long time. Evidence exists of the semi-permanent presence of Mogollon tribes going back nearly to the time of Christ. Pit ruins have been discovered, for instance, around the Leasburg Dam, near Radium Springs, and also near the base of Tortugas Mountain, east of Mesilla. There is even evidence that, around 1300, these people began to build larger, two-story structures, perhaps similar to what the northern Pueblo Indians were building.[i] They seem to have left around 1450, less than fifty years before Columbus first set foot in the New World.

Around the same time as their disappearance, a different sort of Native American began to appear in the Mesilla Valley—the Athabascan tribes of the north, dating back to those people who traveled across the Bering Land Bridge roughly 20,000 years ago. These tribes were nomadic however, wandering through the valley as they foraged and hunted, and would have been predecessors of the Apaches or Navajos.

Soon after Columbus' first landing, Spaniards began to expand into the new lands he had opened up, first across Central and South America, especially in Cortez's conquests of the Aztecs in what would now be southern Mexico and Central America. But, strangely enough, even though the lands of the Mesilla Valley would not be discovered by Europeans until nearly a hundred years after Columbus' arrival, it happened that four explorers came very near to entering and may in fact have entered the Mesilla Valley, as early as the 1530s.

# The Curious Saga of Cabeza de Vaca and Esteban the Moor

By 1513 Spanish explorers led by Ponce de Leon had discovered La Florida and soon thereafter others came to explore this verdant new land. One such group of 600 or so, led by a somewhat notorious conquistador (though perhaps not such a great explorer) named Panfilo de Narvaez, left Spain in 1527. The following year, a little more than half that number arrived on the west coast of Florida, in what would become present-day Tampa Bay. Rather than keeping this group and the ships together, de Narvaez unwisely had himself and around "260 footmen and 40 horsemen" dropped on the shore of the bay.[ii] The ships then left to find better landings to the north. De Narvaez and the men with him would never see the ships again.

Men and horses waded through swamps and were attacked by natives but eventually made it to the area around today's Tallahassee. The ships could not find them, however, so the men were effectively abandoned. Using their spurs and other metal for nails, horse manes for rigging, shirts for sails, the men built rafts, ate their horses, and sailed off into the Gulf of Mexico. They did not fare well, especially when they ran into the strong current off the Mississippi Delta. The rafts were separated and only 80 men reached today's Galveston Island. And then most of those 80 proceeded to die anyway, from starvation and disease. In the end, four men survived, though they did not all know of each others' existence. One of them, who would eventually become their leader, was named Alvar Nunez Cabeza de Vaca. Another of the four was a tall Moorish slave named Esteban, sometimes called the Black Spaniard. However, six years would pass before Cabeza de Vaca and Esteban would meet again and begin their long journey home.[iii]

To survive, Cabeza de Vaca became a trader, a kind of early American entrepreneur, moving goods between native tribes on the western Gulf coast and those inland. In time, realizing he had to try to get back to civilization, or what there was of it somewhere to the west and south, he left the area where he had been trading. Soon, he discovered three other survivors from the expedition, one of whom was Esteban, the slave. The problem was that Esteban had, along with other two men, become a slave again, this time to a native tribe. And then Cabeza de Vaca found himself enslaved as well.

It took another year for the four to escape, but they did, and after what had now been six years in the wilderness, they headed west, on foot, across the land that would one day become Texas. This journey, in short, took another two years, but it's interesting to note that these men, while they were living with the native tribes, had come to be seen as healers of some sort. They had somehow helped several sick natives get better by laying on hands, praying and otherwise "treating" them. Because of this and the word that spread ahead of them, they attracted quite a following of tribal members they encountered, who saw them as holy men. At certain points, their entourage consisted of several thousand Indians.

The men traveled all the way to the west of Mexico, where eventually they encountered Spaniards who barely recognized them as anything other than natives themselves. But in the course this journey, they came across a great river—what would later be called the Rio Grande del Norte—and followed it north as far as present-day El Paso. According to some accounts, the four men came north far enough to actually enter the Mesilla Valley, and so may have crossed the ground upon which the town of Mesilla now sits. In any case, they came very close. This would have been around the year 1535.

# The First Recorded European Presence in the Mesilla Valley

Cabeza de Vaca and Esteban must have heard tales on their journey of great multi-storied pueblo cities to the north. Something in these tales, which were undoubtedly played up for dramatic effect, excited their imaginations and, more important, the imaginations of their Spanish listeners on their return. After the riches that Cortez had gained in his domination of the Aztecs, hopes had run high for years that other such civilizations existed in the new territories that could be exploited as well. In addition, legends of seven mythical cities had circulated in Portugal and Spain for hundreds of years. Now, stories of these unseen northern cities began to fuse with the legends and, fueled by the riches of Cortez, ignited something of a furor—which led quickly to a fervor to begin explorations of this new and unseen land.

These early expeditions would by-pass the Mesilla Valley entirely, contrary to some versions of the history, heading north instead along the western corridor of Mexico and then inland to what is now the eastern part of the state of Arizona, and the across the valley of the Gila River into northern New Mexico. In 1538 Esteban helped guide the first of these, led by a man named Marcos de Niza. It did not go well, and Esteban did not survive. A year later, Francisco Vasquez de Coronado led another expedition along the same route, though some of his men at one point traveled as far south as the northern end of the Mesilla Valley—but they did not enter. Still, although no gold or riches were uncovered, many pueblo cities were discovered in the area of northern New Mexico. Their existence would prove to be very important to the settlement of the unexplored territories and specifically to the eventual presence of Spaniards in the Mesilla Valley. However another 40 years would pass before any serious ventures north were to take place again.

During those years, the Spaniards established silver mines in Mexico, and these gradually spread north into southern present-day Chihuahua. It is possible that expeditions of miners or explorers or potential raiders ventured farther north still, but there is no record of this. As the mines and civilization crept northward, though, eventually a new route began to open from Mexico City up through the Pass to the North, El Paso del Norte.

In 1581, a priest named Fray Augustín Rodriguez obtained official permission to explore the land north of there that was now for the first time being called Nuevo Mexico. Already in his fifties, Rodriguez surrounded himself with younger men—a group of "two other Franciscans . . . nine soldiers [and] . . . sixteen Indians"[iv] – and was drawn by rumors not so much of gold, this time, but of more sophisticated civilized cultures who lived in multi-story houses and dressed in woven clothing, but had yet to be taught the virtues of Catholicism. Rodriguez and his band journeyed north along the Conchos River and then the Rio Grande, encountering fairly primitive tribes along the way, and then, after the Paso del Norte, entered for the first time in recorded history the Mesilla Valley itself. Not much is known of their stay here, but their mission overall was a success, as least as far as establishing new territory and contacting new civilizations was concerned. However, the following year, a party led by two other friars, Bernadino Beltran and Antonio de Espejo, on an unauthorized expedition that also passed through the Mesilla Valley, discovered that Fray Rodriguez and the other priest with him had been martyred.

# Oñate and the Naming of Mesilla

In the years after the Rodriguez and Espejo expeditions, other parties journeyed north through the Mesilla Valley and into the land of the pueblos, but these were all unauthorized. Clearly, there was a building desire to go north again, this time to permanently claim the lands of the "New Mexico." King Felipe II of Spain, who had in 1588 suffered the defeat of his armada at the hands of the English and so was looking for new sources of wealth and land, wanted this to happen as well. It was a matter of finding the right person to lead a new group. Several men petitioned for this right—the possibility of great riches, mineral or otherwise, as well as control over a vast amount of land, were strong enticements. The first serious contender for this right, Juan Bautista de Lomas y Colmenares, over-reached in the demands he presented. When another man, Francisco de Urdinola, was then chosen, Lomas sabotaged his bid by paying witnesses to claim that Urdinola had poisoned Lomas' wife.[v]

The right man in the end turned out to be Don Juan de Oñate, the son of a wealthy mine owner in New Spain, and a military leader and prospector himself. Oñate signed a contract in 1595 with the Viceroy of New Spain that called not for a conquest of the new territory, but rather pacification.[vi] As it would turn out, conquest would probably have been a more accurate word, but the expedition was launched in any case, and it would change forever the land of the pueblo Indians.

This expedition had, from the beginning, something quite different in its aims than earlier ones. Rather than a small group of soldiers and natives and priests looking to conquer and convert, the group that Oñate assembled in Zacatecas at the beginning of 1598 was really the seed of a new society. That was its point. The new world, at least that of the Spanish, was an established civilization at this point. Centered in Mexico City, it had become crowded and dirty, and some people were ready to move on to establish new societies. One of the places that was widely seen as being a potential new home were these territories of the New Mexico to the north. At the end of April of 1598, Oñate crossed the river at El Paso del Norte, into the lower reaches of the Mesilla Valley, and claimed all lands to the north for Spain.

Consequently, the people recruited for this voyage north were generally young, and it was preferred that they have a skill or trade and even a family. Crypto-Jews who had escaped the inquisition in Spain by fleeing to the New World were also anxious now to leave the established Spanish settlements. Oñate, who would become the first governor of New Mexico, could grant to these people titles and land if they stayed in the new territory for five years. (In truth, they were required to stay for five years anyway—if they left early without permission, they were subject to execution.) Friars also would accompany this pilgrimage. So when it left, the group of several hundred had with it "eighty carts and wagons, hundreds of culturally Hispanic and racially mixed people, [and] thousands of head of livestock."[vii]

They would travel up the Rio Grande (also called the Rio del Norte - the River of the North) over the next several months, as far north as present-day Espanola, at the junction of Chama River and the Rio Grande. Eventually the capital of the new territory would move south to Santa Fe. The stories of Oñate's successes and failures, and the cruelties he meted out upon the heads of the natives, are legion and left for a different time.

What is relevant to this account is that, on this first journey north in 1598, Oñate and the expedition that followed him camped not too far north of El Paso del Norte, in what may have once been an Indian village located on a small but high spot near the river that often flooded. It was in the spring, so it is probable that the river was high when they arrived. The name given to this spot by Oñate was the *Trenquel de la Mesilla*. A search of early-modern Spanish, the transitional form of the language between old and modern, spoken at the time of Oñate's expedition, shows that *Trenquel de la Mesilla* actually meant a "military exploration encampment at the little mesa."

A shortening of this ultimately yielded not only the name Mesilla for the future town that would sit on this little mesa above the river, but for the entire valley which opened to its north.

It seems then that Mesilla was the first European name used in New Mexico that would eventually become a town (though that wouldn't happen for another 250 years or so). Though the name *Nuevo Mexico* pre-dated it by nearly 40 years, the mission at Socorro was named after Mesilla, as were the towns of San Juan de los Caballeros in the north and then, later, Santa Fe. Mesilla was the first place Onate encountered on his journey north that was given a name that stuck.

Courtesy of the Palace of the Governors Photo Archives (NMHM/DCA); negative # 006197
"Juan de Onate inscription at El Morro National Monument, New Mexico"; 1930-1940;

"Passed by here the Governor Don Juan De Oñate, from the discovery of the Sea of the South on the 16th of April, 1605." Inscription in rock made by Oñate at El Moro National Monument south of Grants, NM.

# The River and the Royal Road

Oñate, with his priests and soldiers, dominated the natives of the Pueblos, especially those of Acoma, but the colonists worked hard to settle the land as well as to establish missions and to explore. It was the settling that proved most difficult in an inhospitable territory where little could be grown without great effort. Only three years after their arrival, in 1601, Oñate himself left on a new expedition, far to the northeast, that roughly followed the route Coronado had taken. Like Coronado's trek, this mission yielded little. And life in the settlement during his absence did not flourish. By the time Oñate got back, he found that many of the settlers had deserted illegally and headed south again to Mexico. Although there had been some success with mining, especially of silver ore, Oñate was losing a great deal of money. When officials in Mexico City heard the deserters' descriptions of life in the new colony, an investigation was launched[viii]. The combination of the financial failures, the harsh conditions and the inability of settlers to raise enough food, and the treatment of natives led to Oñate being recalled. By 1607, he had resigned his governorship, and by 1612 was banished back to Spain.

Life did not stop in the new land, however. In 1610, Don Pedro de Peralta moved the settlement south to what would become the city of Santa Fe. Construction of the Palace of the Governors (today the oldest continuously occupied public building in the United States) began soon after. More importantly, the route that Oñate and others before him had taken north, was now established.

And so, this is perhaps a good place to pause for a moment—with Sr. Oñate broke and suffering the consequences of his terrible domination of the northern pueblos, the settlement of Santa Fe and the building of the Governor's Palace imminent, the permanent presence of the Spanish Europeans in New Mexico now all but guaranteed despite the difficulties past and future—and say a few words about the river itself, the Rio del Norte, also known as the Rio Grande, and the Mesilla Valley it carved, and about the road that followed them both from Mexico into the north.

The Rio Grande, at over 1800 miles, is the fourth longest river in the U.S., running from the southern Colorado mountains south through New Mexico and along the Texas-Mexico border to the Gulf of Mexico. In New Mexico it follows a geologic construction known as a rift valley, a low area bordered by mountains. Unlike today, the river then was a power, running tranquilly one day then raging and flooding the next, and constantly re-inventing itself as it went.

The Mesilla Valley also looked much different than it does today. Early travelers would have seen patches of cottonwood bosque, or woods, stretching along the broad river bottom and, rising on both sides, hills covered with grass and brush. Old channels, some dried up and filled with silt, traced the river's course from one side of the valley to the other, while flooding continually created steep banks and newer channels through the clay, sand and gravel that composed the valley floor.

The 1600 mile long series of footpaths and trails that Oñate followed north came early on to be called *el Camino Real de Tierra Adentro*, the Royal Road of the Interior Lands. It would prove to be the single most vitally important passage in the early settlement of what would one day become the United States.

Interestingly, it seems to get small consideration today in the national consciousness when it comes to the notion of the founding of the country. Consider the fact that, in 1607, the year of Oñate's resignation, the colonists who established Jamestown, Virginia, popularly considered the founding of what would become America, had just set foot on dry land. The Spanish by that time had already been a presence in New Mexico on and off for seventy years, had been plying the Camino Real for nearly thirty, and had settled the region of the north, however tentatively, ten years earlier. In 1607, it would still be another 13 years before the pilgrims would land at Plymouth Rock.

> Consider too what the Camino Real of the interior brought with it. It was the first European road in America, and for nearly a century the longest. Some of the earliest European settlers in the United States came northward along this trail. The first breeding horses, cattle and sheep entered the American West via this trail. The wheel, gunpowder, written language, iron and Christianity first became established in America through this road.[ix]

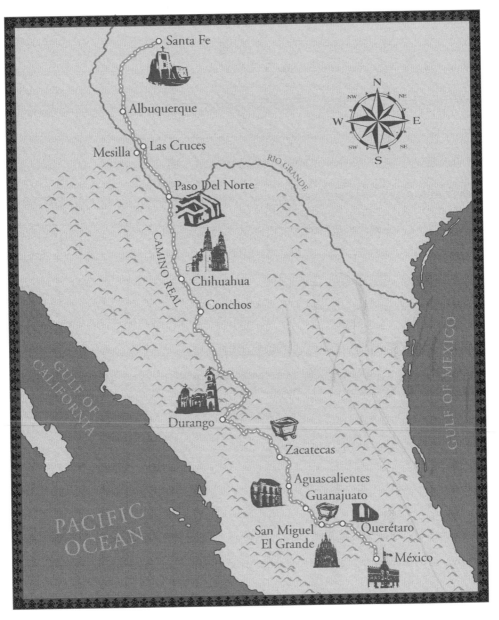

Tu Media Group

The Camino Real, from its beginning in Mexico City
to its terminus in Santa Fe.[x]

# The Journey of Death

Every three years or so, over the century after Oñate's settlement expedition, a new caravan of carretas (wheeled carts) carried loads of supplies from deep in Mexico along the Camino Real through the Mesilla Valley to this new outpost of Spanish civilization. These carretas, built using few tools and no nails or any other metal pieces, were made entirely of wood, including the wheels and axles, and no oils were used to lubricate the wheels as they turned. Imagine being in the caravan day after day for months on end. As the carretas move, your hearing is assaulted by the loud screaming of wheels turning on their axles. The Oñate settlement caravan of 1598 included as many as 70 carretas, with 140 squeaking wheels. These carretas moved best when dry. To cross one of the infrequent rivers or to be drenched during a summer thunderstorm meant that wood would swell so that the wheels could no longer turn on their axles. Pressing on risked the contraption falling apart, and so the only choice was to stop and wait for things to dry. Other than these annoyances, and the fact that the constant loud squawking from the wagon wheels could be heard for miles ahead, alerting possibly hostile natives to your presence, the carretas were a blessing. You could even ride in them, if there was any extra space, and if you did not mind the jolting and bumping.

The older 900 mile route of the Camino Real that stretched from Mexico City north to the silver mines and across a great region of sand dunes until it reached the western bank of the Rio Grande had already been fortified to some degree against raids by native marauders. Now these fortifications began to spread further north along the remaining 700-mile section of road to Santa Fe. But no fortification could protect the colonists from the greatest danger on their journey north after Mesilla—a stretch of land across the center of southern New Mexico called the *Jornada del Muerto*. The term has been translated in various ways, one being the Dead Man's Walk or Journey of the Dead Man, based on the story of a German trader named Gruber who died in 1670 while fleeing across the Jornada. Another translation, simply the Journey of Death,

Esteban Gonnet, circa 1864 [public domain]

An example of a carreta.

derives from the words of the governor of the territory in the late 1600s, Antonio de Otermin, after the deaths of many Santa Fe colonists who were forced to retreat to the south across the Jornada after a Pueblo Indian uprising.

In these great journeys north and south, the Mesilla Valley played a vital role in the survivability of the Jornada crossings. Spanning the distance between the crossing of the river from west bank to east at El Paso del Norte and the Jornada, the valley served as a relatively lush oasis. Its upper end was the last plentiful source of water before entering the long arid stretch or, conversely, the first relief when coming out of it. Most traffic seems to have moved along the east bank, in any case, and through the area where Las Cruces would one day stand, though this was a difficult road though in places because of arroyos and sand hills. The trail along the river began to become impassable at the area of the present day Radium Springs, also the location of the remains of the 19th century Fort Selden. This was the Robledo Crossing and the often-used camping spot there was the Robledo Paraje. Parajes were established all along the Camino Real, of course. This particular one was named for Pedro Robledo, who with his sons accompanied Juan de Oñate on that maiden mission in 1598, and died on this spot. You can see a marker with this information in front of the Fort Selden ruins.

It seems counterintuitive that the voyagers from Mexico would leave the safety and relative comfort of the river to venture more than 90 miles across arid desert, where the few springs along the way proved inadequate for the number of people and animals in the caravans. But it's easy and rather fascinating to see why for yourself. If you head east from Mesilla on the Avenida, then turn left at Valley Drive, you'll be on state route 185. This takes you north out of Las Cruces on a scenic drive along the river. In only about fifteen miles you'll come to Fort Selden Road, also the location of the turnoff away from the river for the Robledo Crossing. If you continue on 185 much farther, you can immediately see why the old route turned away here. The river begins a broad turn to the west, though with many sharper curves in both directions, and from the relatively flat open passage you've been driving, the terrain narrows very suddenly and you find yourself between large outcroppings on one side and mountains on the other. It is almost as if you have entered a tunnel, and it is clear that it would have been more difficult for horse- or burro-drawn carts to have passed much further, especially on the east side of the river.

There is another spot a few miles further north, near present-day Rincon, called the San Diego paraje. Some caravans apparently managed to stay with the river to this point, and then cut away. This was the last contact with the river northbound caravans could have had. After this the river remained impassable, or vanished entirely where it flowed underground, for a long ways north, until eventually it curved back and regained its route due north around today's Bosque del Apache wildlife preserve.

The solution was clear—follow the established Indian trails that lead to the north across the desert where the ground was hard and relatively flat and open. You can see this too, if you're driving and care to go a little farther north.

Head east on Fort Selden Road, until you come to Interstate 25, and then north another 17 miles to the Upham exit (this is near the San Diego Paraje). Turn right, east, when you exit. The world seems to end rather suddenly here; as soon as you leave the exit ramp, you'll find yourself on a wide unmarked gravel road with nothing else around you but the land and the sky. But if you drive just a little farther, you'll be able to see almost immediately to your left the vast open passage that the caravans followed. It is rather stunning, bordered by the Caballo Mountains to the left and smaller peaks to the east that include Point of Rocks, one of the signposts the caravans looked for.

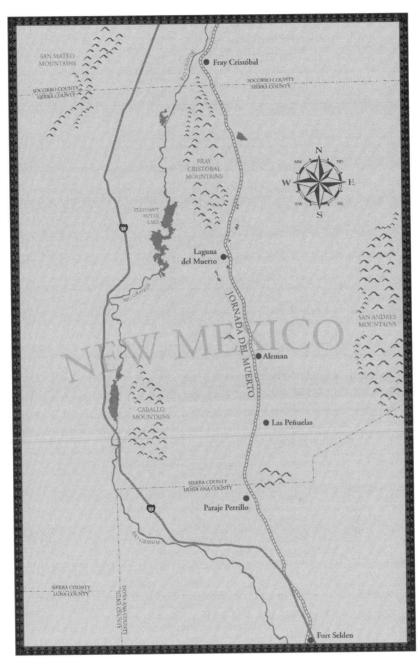

Tu Media Group

The Jornada del Muerto in relation to today's river and landmarks, including I-25. Of course, when it was in use, the reservoirs at Elephant Butte and Caballo were not there, and in fact the river disappeared altogether in places along that section of its route.

# Revolt, Retreat, Recapture—The Spanish Come To Stay

Much could be said about the Spanish colonies in and around Santa Fe during the 17th century, but little that mattered during most of that period happened around Mesilla or in the Mesilla Valley other than the passing through of the great freight wagon trains twice every three years (once in each direction). Instead of the small all-wooden carts that brought Oñate's caravans and those following in the early years, these wagons were built for bulk. With iron-rimmed wheels, they carried two tons each and were pulled by eight mules. There were usually 32 of them in a train, and herds of livestock went with them as well, as did armed guards.[xi] Coming north, they brought more friars, building materials, clothing and other supplies. They did not return to Mexico empty, either.

It's almost certain that these caravans stopped to camp at the small plateau called the Trenquel de la Mesilla. In the immediate area, marked by arroyos, flooding, etc, there was not another obvious resting place given the marshiness of the surrounding landscape.

But life in Santa Fe was not shaping up as perhaps had first been imagined. For one thing a conflict had arisen between the governors of the new territory and the friars, especially during and after the gubernatorial term of Captain Don Luis de Rosas, beginning in 1637. He and the Franciscans were in virtual war with each other, leading to a schism in the Spanish community.[xii] And there was not a very large Spanish community to begin—a peak of probably 2500 settlers, including Mexican natives who had come north, and almost all of whom had been born in this territory. Migration north had largely ceased other than the influx of more Friars. When the population did increase it was through procreation, and not all of the babies were purely Spanish. The colony had never become a profitable enterprise for the king of Spain. In fact it lost money. But that was not the point. The tenor, the real reason, for its existence came to be more about religion than trade or mining or establishing new societies. Of course the native Pueblos were in the middle of this, as slaves and property, but also more than that. These natives were also the source of income, and, most importantly, the objects of conversion, the souls to be saved even if it cost them their lives.

In Spain at this time the Inquisition was raging. And just because the New World lay some distance away, it was not spared from this scrutiny, aimed at, among others, crypto-Jews, both in Mexico City and those who had migrated northward to escape that persecution. The power or at least influence and effect of the friars had spread widely. Their missions were flung across an area from Socorro to Taos and far to the west and east—covering perhaps 6000 square miles. Tens of thousands of baptisms of Pueblo Indians were taking place. The Pueblos, in addition to being subject to paying tributes and forced into labor, had their own religion disparaged by the Spanish even to the point that their kivas were burned and religious objects destroyed.[xiii] The fact that the Pueblos vastly outnumbered the Spanish apparently did not give the friars or governors pause. Or perhaps it did, because for many years their heavy-handed control of the natives kept the forces of dissatisfaction in check.

But in 1680 the Indians had had enough. 6,000 warriors attacked the Spanish Missions from Socorro to Taos, killing 21 missionaries and 400 colonists before the remaining 2,000, along with members of the Tigua and Piro tribes, fled to the south, back across the Jornada del Muerto. It was this retreat that led the governor of the territory, himself grievously wounded, to write about the Journey of Death. Some 2500 souls gathered at the Paraje Fra Cristobal, near Socorro, the northern entrance to the Jornada. Slightly less than 2000 reached the southern end of the Mesilla Valley, where the obvious campsite was the raised spot that would one day hold Mesilla itself. Their goal, the closest settlement further south, was Juarez at El Paso del Norte.[xiv]

In fact, this influx helped to establish Juarez as a city (encompassing both today's Ciudad de Juarez and El Paso) and soon after a fort was built there for protection of its inhabitants.

An interesting aside to this story, which would have ramifications many years later, has to do with the mission that was built at present-day Juarez around 1650, years before the construction of the fort at Paso del Norte. This mission was constructed for the benefit of indigenous tribes in the area – the Manso, who were living in the Mesilla Valley when the Spanish first came through, and the Tiwa. But the first inhabitants were actually Piro Indians from farther north, Christian converts brought in by the Franciscans. These Piro were kept separate from the other tribes. In subsequent years, other tribes, Tiwa and Tompiros, came to live at the mission as well due to drought and Apache attacks. A couple of years after the native revolt, when the Spanish first tried to re-take New Mexico, they ended up capturing another group of Tiwo and Piro at Isleta, and brought them back to Paso del Norte as well, though they were placed in new missions. In the early 1700s another tribe, the

Jano, were settled in the Guadalupe mission as well.

This mingling and settling of tribes, especially the ones at the Guadalupe Mission, would eventually become the Pueblo Indians of Guadalupe, effectively a new tribe that would maintain an importance presence in the area, particularly in the Mesilla Valley, once it began to be settled and through to the present day.[xv]

Esteban Gonnet, circa 1864 [public domain]

Caravans similar to the freight wagons of the Spanish.

# An Old Land Made New

The revolt and devastating retreat was a blow to the young community that should by rights have been fatal. The Pueblos had done what no other native group ever had—taken back their territory and ousted the interlopers. But the blow was not fatal. The Spanish ultimately were not to be denied this land, this *Nuevo Mexico*.

It would take 12 years but a new governor from Spain named Don Diego de Vargas would lead a Reconquista. In 1692, he and 200 troops surrounded Santa Fe and negotiated a peace with the Pueblos. In 1693, de Vargas organized re-colonization, bringing in 70 families and 18 friars. The city was re-established as the capital of the territory, and the Franciscans commenced reclaiming the abandoned missions in the area. Though there would be other revolts, from this point forward the territory would remain inhabited by the Spanish and their descendants.

In 1706, the city of Albuquerque was founded.

By 1752, the number of Spanish settlers in New Mexico had increased to 3402.

And in 1792, 100 years after the re-establishment of Santa Fe and seventeen years after the United States declared its independence from England, French traders crossed the Mississippi and journeyed across Texas and into Santa Fe.

By 1800, the number of Spanish in New Mexico hit 24,000.

Gradually the New Mexico territory, which had once been the bastion of Native Americans and then of Spanish immigrants, saw a new people begin to arrive. For some years, French traders working for U.S. companies had been wandering into Santa Fe. But in 1804, with the accomplishment of the Louisiana Purchase, the territory of the United States had spread suddenly drastically west, even encroaching now on a part of what would become the state of New Mexico.

Explorations from the east began in earnest with the Lewis and Clark expedition in that same year. The Spanish were not only aware of these interlopers but even at one point sent troops north to try to disrupt the exploration, fearing (correctly) that these new foreigners would eventually try to take this land. The attempt failed. But not long later, in early 1807, they did manage to intercept and capture an expedition in southern Colorado led by Zebulon Pike. Pike and his men were taken south as far as Chihuahua and held for several months, though they were not treated badly and in fact learned much about the mapping the Spanish had done of the southwest, and also of the building discontent between the new country of Mexico and its Spanish rulers.[xvi]

And then, in 1821, the Santa Fe Trail was established, connecting Franklin, Missouri (about a hundred miles east of Kansas City) directly to the plaza in downtown Santa Fe.[2] It would become the first major supply route into the area after the Camino Real. The link now to the East, to the English and French and those who would come after, was irreversibly established.

New Mexico had become a thriving colony and a destination. It and its older southern sister, Mexico, were still colonies of Spain. But that was about to change.

i Scott E. Fritz, "Mercantile Crossroads: The Mesilla Valley Prior to 1870," *Southern New Mexico Historical Review*, V, no. 1 (1998): 37-40.

ii John L. Kessel, *Spain in the Southwest*, (Norman, OK: University of Oklahoma Press, 2002): 17

iii Donald E. Chipman, "ESTEVANICO," *Handbook of Texas Online* , accessed August 22, 2013. Published by the Texas State Historical Association, http://www.tshaonline.org/handbook/online/articles/fes08

iv Bannon, John Francis, *The Spanish Borderlands Frontier, 1513-1821* (Albuquerque NM: University of New Mexico Press, 1974): 30-32

v Kessel, *Spain*, 71

vi Kessel, *Spain*, 73

vii Kessel, *Spain*, 75

viii NM Office State Historian, "Juan de Oñate." Accessed September 7, 2013. http://www.newmexicohistory.org/filedetails.php?fileID=312.

ix Douglas Preston, The Royal Road: El Camino Real from Mexico City to Santa Fe, (Albuquerque: University of New Mexico Press, 1998), 4.

x Digital enhancement of all maps by Tu Media Group unless otherwise noted.

xi Kessel, *Spain*, 113

xii Grace Meredith, "Rosas, Luis de." New Mexico Office of the State Historian, Accessed September 24, 2013. http://www.newmexicohistory.org/filedetails.php?fileID=23487

xiii Jack Wintz, "The Old Missions of New Mexico," AmericanCatholic.org, Accessed September 24, 2013. http://www.americancatholic.org/messenger/oct1998/feature1.asp.

xiv El Camino Real International Heritage Center, "Jornada del Muerto: The Journey of Death." Accessed September 9, 2013. http://www.caminorealheritage.org/jornada/jornada.htm.

xv Henry Torres, unpublished paper, April, 2014, based on following sources: *The Southwestern Journals of Adolph F. Bandelier*, edited and annotated by Charles H. Lange and Carrol I. Riley; Beckett, Patrick H., and Terry L. Corbett, *The Manso Indians*, COAS Pub. & Research, 1992, *Tortugas*, COAS, Pub. & Research, 1990; Hurt, Wesley R. *Tortugas, an Indian Village in Southern New Mexico*, El Palacio, April 1952 pp. 104-122.

xvi John Buescher, "Trailing Lewis and Clark," teachinghistory.org, Accessed October 4, 2013. http://teachinghistory.org/history-content/ask-a-historian/24290

xvii SantaFeTrailResearch.com, "Santa Fe Trail Research." Last modified 10 01, 2008. Accessed September 30, 2013. http://www.santafetrailresearch.com.

# Part II

## Settlers Come to the Valley . . .

# First Settlements

It was during the period from the late 18th into the early 19th centuries that the Mesilla Valley itself, always a highway, never a home, still lush and untamed, fed and divided by the wild erratic river, began to see the first suggestions of permanent settlement. The first land granted by the Spanish, sometime before 1790, was called the Santa Teresa Grant, and was, according to the New Mexico Office of the State Historian, "a four-league tract of land situated on the west bank of the Rio Grande River, the southeast corner of which was located about seven miles northwest of El Paso del Norte, Mexico, [that] was granted to Francisco Garcia, the military commandant of El Paso del Norte, by the Lieutenant Governor of Nueva Viscaya."[xviii] Other sources claim slightly different information. Maude Elizabeth McFie (Bloom), for instance, in her wonderful 1903 senior history thesis for the state college at Las Cruces, states that the grant was actually made as early as 1768 to a man named Joaquin Mestas, though this was not confirmed.[xix]

The second, the Bracito Grant [see map, page 47 ], was made in the early 19th century. Again according to Maude Elizabeth McFie (Bloom), "the earliest settlement in the valley of which I have accurate information, is that of a ranch owned by Don Juan Antonio Garcia, located upon what is now called the Bracito Grant, for he was the original founder of that grant."[xx] Indians were a great threat to settlers in the area and, as McFie points out, in the summer of 1822 all inhabitants of the ranch were driven off. But the settlers came still, if slowly. McFie mentions a man named Buenavides who " . . . had a wooden house at Cañoncito, a small place down the valley between 15 and 18 miles above El Paso . . . " and who had apparently dug an irrigation ditch. This was around 1813.[xxi]

The descendants who were living on the Santa Teresa land were also forced at this same time to abandon the ranch, at least temporarily. Neither tract of land would be permanently occupied until the middle of the century. Still, though the valley could hardly be called settled, inhabitation had begun, and would only grow as time went on. But this land, this rich valley, lay without its knowing at the eye of brewing territorial storm that would spin out in one way or another over many years, really all the way up to the granting of statehood in 1912.

# The Free Countries of Mexico . . .

A storm had begun already in 1785 with the rioting of native parishioners near Mexico City at the rumor of the replacement of a statue of the Virgin Mary.[xxii] As the Spanish had foisted Catholicism on the New World, so Catholicism would, in its way, lie at least in part at the roots of the Spanish losing it. The roots of this riot and of what would happen over the next 40 or so years lay deep, of course, and also across the ocean in the homeland. Spain itself was in great turmoil at the turn into the 19th century, with rioting there too, upheaval next door with the French Revolution, the Napoleonic wars and even a takeover of the Spanish throne at one point by Josef Bonaparte. Spain's attentions were, one might say, focused in other places than the lands of Mexico, old or new. The ruling classes in the New World had always been Spanish of course, but the natives, as they say, were restless and certain elements of the ruling parties and the intelligentsia began to see this unrest as a possible way toward independence.

One such member was a priest named Miguel Hidalgo y Costilla. The stuff of revolution is often modest in its beginnings. A statue of the Virgin Mary. Tea in a Boston Harbor. In the case of Don Hidalgo, the issue was grapes. This accounting comes from another historical text, by Fayette Robinson, published in 1847: Hidalgo was a quiet bookish man with a parish in the small town of Dolores, where he established a silk enterprise for the people, and then moved on to a vineyard, with an eye toward the town making its own wine, as well as many other goods. The Spanish had come to the New World for its riches, and that remained the case—they took whatever bounty they could out, and imported whatever they could to be sold locally, the profits returning to Spain. The making of wine then by Mexican locals was forbidden and Hidalgo's vineyards were destroyed.[xxiii] Rather than cow him, this affront spurred Hidalgo into relationships with other revolutionaries. In 1810, they amassed a kind of army of several thousand and began attacking Spanish holdings right up to the edge of Mexico City before retreating. Later, the size of this revolutionary force reached 80,000. Eventually though Hidalgo and the others fled north into the province of Texas, until they were finally captured and executed in 1811.

But the seeds were sown; the mechanism in place. It would only be another ten years before Mexico gained its independence from Spain, 329 years after Columbus's arrival, and 211 years after The Palace of Governor's was built.

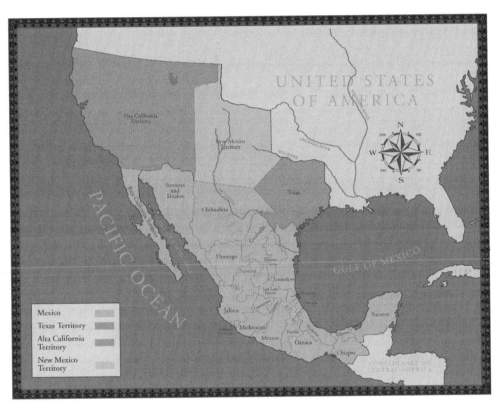

Tu Media Group

Mexico and its political divisions shortly after its independence, around 1824.

# ... and of Texas.

Texas was one of the northern provinces of Mexico at the time of its independence, but people from further north had been moving down into this vast land and settling it. Fearing what this might lead to, Mexico actually tried to discourage northerners from migrating south (an interesting if ironic twist on the situation today), but of course they could not be stopped. In 1835 Texas settlers began to revolt, and in 1836 declared its independence which spurred a war with Mexico. The Mexican general and dictator Santa Anna led forces north to quell the revolution, culminating in the loss of some 500 lives at and after the battle of the Alamo, though ultimately resulting, after a daring charge in which outnumbered Texans took Santa Anna's forces by surprise, in the capture of Santa Anna himself. Of this last encounter, in April, 1836, Santa Anna is known to have said, "So sudden and fierce was the enemy's charge that the earth seemed to move and tremble."

And so, in that year, Texas became for a short time anyway a country in its own right, recognized first by the United States and then by England, France and Belgium. It then promptly declared that the western frontier of the Republic extended all the way to Rio Grande, and so included the eastern half of New Mexico as well parts of what would become Colorado, Kansas, Oklahoma and Wyoming. Mexico disputed this, since it still controlled all lands to the west of the new country of Texas. If Texas' new boundary claim was allowed to stand, Mexico would lose a great portion of its New Mexico territory including the now ancient Mexican city of Santa Fe.

Five years later, after trading posts were established, Texas President Mirabeau Lamar sent a group of military and business people west into this disputed area. It was known as the Texas Santa Fe Expedition, and was designed to not only strengthen Texas' claim to the land but to win over people living in that territory so that they would want to declare themselves a part of Texas. The group comprised about 300 people, including three commissioners empowered to negotiate with residents of Santa Fe as well as a newspaperman named George Wilkins Kendall.[xxiv] Kendall is interesting because he would later write a book about this experience, which went badly wrong when the expedition was intercepted by Mexican troops. After surrendering their arms under the false pretense that they would be released, all were taken prisoner and marched south into Mexico. This act of course did little to improve the already strained relations between Mexico and the United States (and in fact these disputed lands would lie at the base of the war that was to come in the not too distant future). But it's interesting that this sad group, many of whom died on that trek, is picked up again by our friend Maude Elizabeth McFie (Bloom), who mentions it and Mr. Kendall's book when giving an account of early settlements in the Mesilla Valley. Of this time, in 1840, she says, citing Kendall's book, that, "he states definitely that there was no settlement between Socorro and El Paso."[xxv]

To this point the Mesilla Valley, notwithstanding the grants mentioned above, had still not been permanently settled. But that was now very quickly to change.

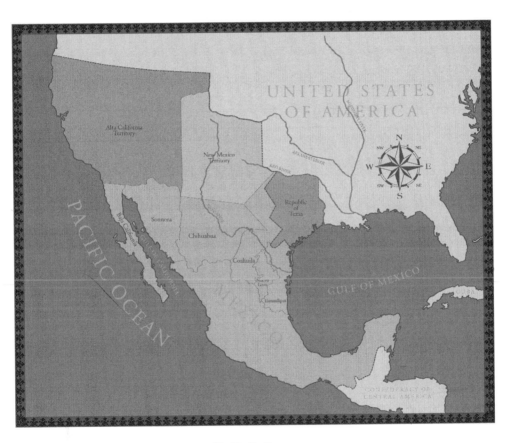

Tu Media Group

Map of Mexico after Texas secession, according to 1836 treaty signed by Mexico. This was Mexico's understanding of the land it had ceded to Texas.

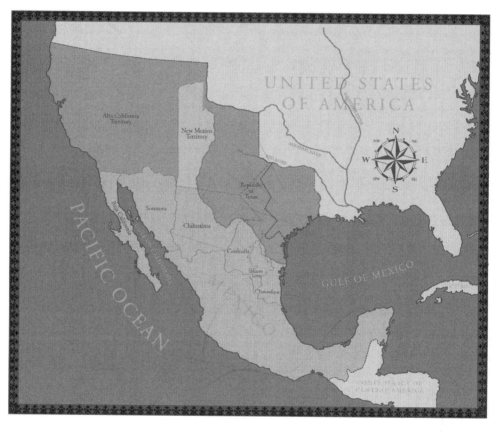

Tu Media Group

Map of Texas published in 1837 after its independence claiming slightly more land than Mexico thought it was giving up.

# The Doña Ana Bend Colony—First Town in the Mesilla Valley

By the early 1840s, as we have seen from the testimony of George Kendall, there were still no permanent settlements in the Mesilla Valley, the tentative settlers on the early grants having been forced off repeatedly by Indian attacks and uprisings. The valley was at that time deeply within the still very hostile Apache lands, at the heart of the coming Indian wars that would rage until the 1880s. But El Paso del Norte to the south was a quickly growing city, and the farm lands around it were becoming insufficient to support it for much longer. And so, even as the prisoner George Kendall marched through the Valley and saw no settlements, the changes to rectify that absence were already happening. After some false starts, the governor of the Mexican state of Chihuahua gave permission to the Prefect of El Paso del Norte to grant land near a fertile bend in the Rio Bravo del Norte (aka the Rio Grande) in the center of the Mesilla Valley to a group of 115 settlers. The grant stretched some 13 or so miles along the river, encompassing the land that not only the town of Doña Ana would rest upon, but also those of Las Cruces, Mesilla, Mesilla Park and Tortugas.

It wouldn't be until early 1843 [xxvi] that 33 of them would establish the first colony, named Doña Ana, on this land. And even then success was hardly assured. By the spring of that year the number of settlers had already dwindled to 14 and the Chihuahuan governor sent an emergency detachment of soldiers to protect them.[xxvii] The state wanted this colony to succeed, but living conditions, especially the frequent Indian attacks, threatened to dictate otherwise.

Maude Elizabeth McFie (Bloom) tells us that, upon one visit, a Mexican official was met by only four settlers because the others had no clothes to wear and so were hiding. He then gave them military uniforms and a horse and mules. They lived in adobe huts and their planting implements were largely wooden. In addition, only half of the settlers could work at any time because the other half had to hold lookout for Indians.  However, they were diligent and hard workers and by that spring of 1843 an 8 mile acequia stretched from the river through the town  of Doña Ana.[xxviii]

The settlement would be moved soon after that to the present day location of Doña Ana, but that first acequia in the Mesilla Valley would of course prove to be a harbinger of many more to come.

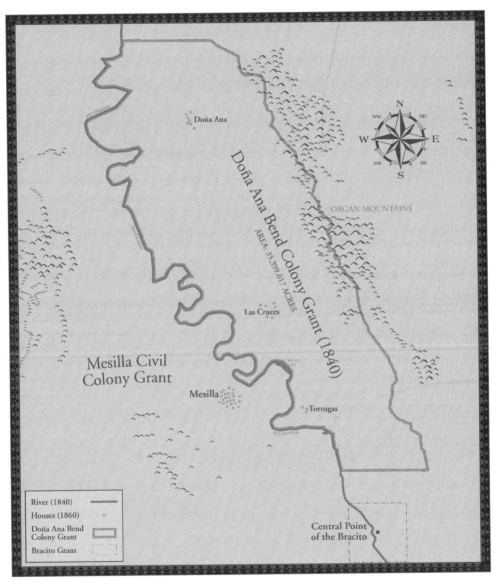

Tu Media Group

Overview of the Doña Ana Bend Colony Grant, the Mesilla Civil Colony Grant and a portion of the original Barcito grant.

# War!

The U.S. had had designs on the Texas territory, especially the eastern portion of it, since the Louisiana Purchase of 1803. Andrew Jackson especially saw it as an extension of the new American south, a rightful part of the country. And in the late 1830s Jackson was already considering war with Mexico due to this desire and to hard feelings over Texas' independence and the United States' recognition of it. War did not of course happen then, but tensions remained, as did the desire for land. President Polk, in his first Cabinet meeting in 1845, announced that California's fine Pacific ports were the prime goal of his Presidency.

What also remained, as far as Mexico's claim to lands north and west of the Rio Grande was concerned, was the fact that it was already involved in another kind of war—spread across the southwest but centered, one could argue, along the banks of the Rio Grande as it passed through the Mesilla Valley. And that was the implicit war that had been under way for years against the Native Americans of the southwest and northern Mexico. From the time of the passage of the great Spanish caravans along the Camino Real, life across the region, but especially along the river, had been very difficult because of the aggressive warlike behavior of the Indians. In New Mexico it was the Apaches; across much of Texas it was the Comanches. As we've already seen, settled land had to be abandoned again and again because of uprisings and raids. Travelers were attacked. Life in the fledging settlement of Doña Ana was a constant state of alert.

The U.S. blamed Mexico for this state of affairs. The land had been under Spanish and then Mexican control for hundreds of year, yet the problem of the Indians had never been solved. Mexico, in a sense, it was believed, didn't deserve this territory. "Along with cowardice, American observers blamed Mexico's Indian problem on Mexican sloth, physical weakness, and stupidity . . . By 1844, most of America's intellectual and political elites thought of themselves as belonging to a separate and superior Anglo Saxon race destined to take possession of North America from other 'retrograde' races".[xxix] If the Native Americans were savages, prevailing beliefs held, then the Mexicans were mongrels. The land needed to be taken or bought, whichever it took.

Combine this xenophobia with the belief in manifest destiny, the flat desire for more land, and the on-going instability of the Mexican government along with the financial debt it already owed many U.S. citizens and you have the fuel that would launch a war. And then when, in 1845, the U.S. annexed Texas, with it it's claim to all lands north and east of the Rio Grande and simultaneously granted it statehood, war was virtually guaranteed.

In that same year of 1845, Polk sent General Zachary Taylor west with an army to the banks of the Rio Grande to enforce that river as the Texas border and also, probably, as a provocation and a visible threat—the iron fist in the velvet glove. For late in that same year, before any hostilities would occur, Polk, who had believed for some time that he could simply buy the territory north of the Rio Grande and west to the Pacific, sent negotiators to Mexico City to offer money. The U.S. would pay $25 million for the territory, plus forgive of Mexico's remaining 3 million or so in debt. It didn't work—Mexico refused outright.

The provocation though was more successful. In the spring of 1846, as Taylor's force worked its way west, U.S. soldiers were killed. That was all the spark the tinder box needed. Polk, claiming that Mexico had crossed the boundary of the United States, pushed Congress to declare and finance a war. Though this was opposed by most Whigs (and would become one of the pillars underlying the U.S. Civil War to come), Congress went along. War was declared May 13, 1846.

# Colonel Doniphan Rests at
# the Brazito Paraje

Given the size of the territory at stake, it makes sense that the war itself would play out over a large area. Battles sites ranged from northern California to the Gulf Coast and across the vast landscape in between. And since New Mexico lay in the center of all of this, it isn't surprising that the war found its way here, too. What is perhaps surprising is that only one major battle occurred anywhere in the territory, and what fighting there was lasted only a few hours. The brevity of the conflict though should not belie its importance.

If you're standing in the town of Mesilla, you are less than ten miles from a historical marker identifying yet another paraje along the Camino Real, this one called Brazito. It stands just north of the town of Vado at the three-way intersection of NM 478 (Main Street in Las Cruces) and NM 227 (Vado Road - also reached by the exit from Interstate 10), in a barren strip of dirt between the end of the road and the railroad track. The spot, once perched on the banks of a broad curve in the then fervent river where islands had formed, was heavily shaded and so was a natural place for travelers to camp. But that fact is not all the marker commemorates. It notes also that this is the location of a clash fought on Christmas Day, 1846, called the Battle of Brazito. And that battle marked a turn in the war.

Colonel Alexander Doniphan, a lawyer by profession, and the regiment he commanded, had come across the western portion of what then composed the United States as part of the much larger force of around 2500, the American Army of the West, led by General Stephen Kearney. This army reached Santa Fe in August prepared to fight for control of the New Mexico territory, to battle for the capital of Santa Fe. But to most everyone's surprise there was no battle. There were not in fact any Mexican forces remaining in the city by the time the Americans arrived. Many New Mexicans, it seemed, were not unhappy at this turn of events, although some Mexican settlers did flee south and settled in Doña Ana and the Mesilla Valley. (A garrison of Mexican Troops was at one point stationed at the future site of Mesilla as well—the best campsite in the immediate area and in use for over 200 years.) The stars and stripes went up in the Santa Fe plaza and so, for the first time in history, flew over the New Mexico. Claiming such a huge territory with the taking of one city was of course a different matter than actually controlling it. And so there was work to be done. It started with installing a new government and new laws and then addressing the Indian problems around and to the north of Santa Fe. Late in the year though it was time to begin stretching out across the broader territory to clear it as well and then to join the more pitched battles in Mexico. And so Doniphan led his regiment south along the river and across the Jornada, exactly as the Spaniards had done before them for hundreds of years.

When they emerged, they rested at the tiny settlement of Doña Ana, the men singularly unimpressed with that humble place and the crude mud buildings that had been erected. Word had circulated of a large Mexican force not too far to the south but Doniphan pushed on. Aside from a skirmish between scouts, not much happened as they continued to the Brazito Paraje, which they reached on the afternoon of Christmas day. It was quiet and it was a holiday and the men were preparing for a bit of a break. "The setting was one of serenity, the mood was laid back, and the actions of the Americans as they sat about their camp did not even remotely resemble alarm. Doniphan and his fellow officers sat down in the shade of a cottonwood and took up a game of cards, with a prized horse as the object being wagered upon".[xxx]

But a Christmas rest was not to be had. A dust cloud signaled the approach of a much larger force of Mexican soldiers that had been based at the Paso del Norte (El Paso). The Americans were both outnumbered and outgunned, the Mexicans having artillery as well as infantry. There was a pause before the battle in which an emissary from the Mexican side insulted Doniphan by demanding a surrender. Doniphan, though angered, held his fire and soon the Mexicans came in shooting both balls and artillery rounds from hundreds of yards away. Doniphan checked his men, and they held in the face of what must have seemed an impending cataclysm until the enemy was only fifty yards away. And then they let loose. The effect was profound. The enemy force turned and fled, and after a few more skirmishes in which the Americans captured the enemy artillery, the battle was over. Not one American soldier was killed.

The victory marked a couple of important milestones. It was the last time Mexican forces would ever hold authority in the New Mexico territory and ". . . the first large body of Americans ever to enter the Mesilla Valley".[xxxi] A presence that would continue, of course, to the present day.

Doniphan entered El Paso soon after. The few residents in that part of Mexico, exhausted and thinned by the constant battles with Native Americans, offered little resistance to the American incursion. Much of the countryside by that point had been abandoned. Doniphan would go on the following spring, of 1848, to occupy the city of Chihuahua. The war would effectively end later that year when U.S. troops under General Winfield Scott, who had landed at Veracruz in March, would by September take Mexico City.

# That Crazy River

The conclusion of the war with Mexico would mark a profound change for-ever after in the direction and development of the Mesilla Valley. As a result of treaties, settlements, new modes of transportation, political upheavals, and so forth, the area would flourish even as it changed again and yet again. But to really be able to picture the effects of the events that were to come, one must first have a picture of the river at the time—or perhaps it is more accurate to say the rivers. Because the river was itself one of the main agents of change and upheaval, even while it served as a metaphor for the change and unpre-dictability that would mark the area around the coming settlements of Mesilla and Las Cruces.

It its modern history, the Rio Grande, as we know it today, has gone by many names. Early Spaniards referred to it as the Rio del Norte and the Rio Turbio (Turbulent River), the Río de Nuestra Señora de la Concepción and the Río Guadalquivir. Oñate is thought to have been the first to call it the Rio Grande, though it was more commonly referred to by the Spanish at that time as the Rio Bravo del Norte or just the Rio Bravo. It is still called that in Mexico today. [xxxii]

Reference has already been made to the fact that the area along the river in these early years and into the 20th century was much wilder and more over-grown than it is today, and that it was prone to flooding and rerouting. It's interesting to note too that even before there were many settlers in the valley taking water off into acequias, the river was also known to disappear. "The records show that in 1851 it was dry as far north as Socorro, New Mexico. Again in 1860 or 1861 it was dry in the Mesilla Valley, and 1879 was the driest year of record prior to 1889 . . . "[xxxiii] There were however also oxbow lakes around what is now Mesilla as well.

But the most notable feature of the river one needs to know to envision the evolution of Mesilla after the war with Mexico is the fact that, from sometime around 1840, it ran to the east of the plateau where Mesilla would be founded.

That is to say, it ran between what is now the modern day city of Las Cruces and the town of Mesilla. This would remain the case until another series of serious floods from 1862 - 1865 would reroute the river once again, splitting it so that, in 1863, Mesilla would actually become an island, bounded by the river on both sides, and then after 1884-85 settling in a single bed to the west of Mesilla where it would remain. Mesilla would be, at least intermittently, an island for a period of twenty years.

The old riverbed to the east can still be seen. If you begin at the south side of the plaza on Calle de Parian (which becomes Boutz when it crosses Hwy 28), and head east, you will come to a dip in the road soon after you pass out of town. This is the old riverbank, and so as you continue you are entering the riverbed. To your left, you'll see an old house on the crest. This was the original adobe ferryman's residence on the western bank. Immediately beyond this you then enter an area that was bounded by an oxbow. Shortly after that you encounter another dip, which means you're crossing the river again (see 2nd map below).

The ramifications of these old channels and their alterations would have much to do with both the founding and the development and future of Mesilla, as we shall see.

The following two maps are of modern day Mesilla and Las Cruces with the present route of the river (in pale blue) and the 1844 route of the river (in darker blue) superimposed. One can see that it would have crossed Valley drive in several places, extended almost as far east as the intersection of El Paseo Road and University Avenue, then meandered back and forth across south Main Street for some distance south of town.

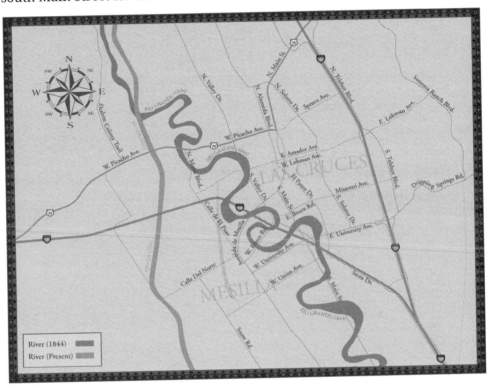

Tu Media Group

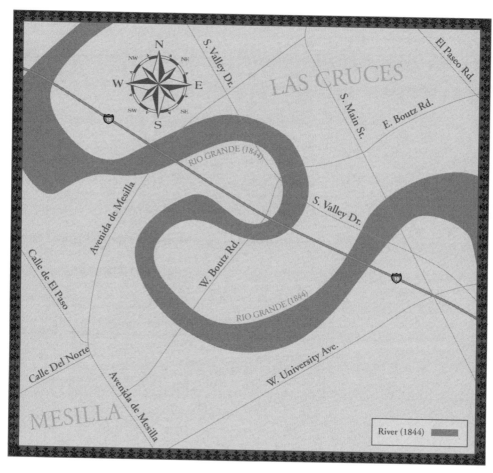

Tu Media Group

A close up showing the route on Boutz Road heading east from Mesilla. It would actually have crossed the river three times.

[xviii] J.J. Bowden, J.J. , "Santa Teresa Grant," New Mexico Office of the State Historian. Accessed October 17, 2013. http://www.newmexicohistory.org/filedetails. php?fileID=24672

[xix] Maude Elizabeth McFie (Bloom), *A History of the Mesilla Valley - 1903*, (Las Cruces, NM: Jo Tice Bloom, 1998), 15

[xx] McFie, *History*, 15

[xxi] McFie, *History*, 2

[xxii] Christon Archer, *The Birth of Modern Mexico, 1780-1824*, (Wilmington, DE: Scholarly Resources Inc., 2003), 41

[xxiii] Fayette Robinson, *Mexico and Her Military Chieftains*, (Philadelphia: E.H. Butler & Co., 1847), 30. http://books.google.com/books?id=gRhMAAAAMAAJ&p rintsec=frontcover&dq=mexico and her military chieftains robinson&hl=en&s a=X&ei=RHxVUr2zIMq7qAGduICIDg&ved=0CC0Q6AEwAA

[xxiv] F.S. Donnell, "When Texas Owned New Mexico to the Rio Grande," Accessed October 15, 2013, http://www.newmexicohistory.org/filedetails. php?fileID=24108

[xxv] McFie, *History*, 2

[xxvi] Bowden, J.J., "Doña Ana Bend Colony Grant," New Mexico Office of the State Historian. Accessed October 19, 2013. http://www.newmexicohistory.org/file-details.php?fileID=24678

[xxvii] Bowden, *Doña Ana*

McFie, *History*, 16

[xxix] Brian DeLay, *War of a Thousand Deserts*, (New Haven: Yale University Press, 2008), 245

[xxxi] William S. Kiser, *Turmoil on the Rio Grande*, (College Station, TX: Texas A&M University Press, 2011), 16

Kiser, *Turmoil*, 31

[xxxii] Leon C. Metz, "RIO GRANDE," *Handbook of Texas Online*, published by the Texas State Historical Association. Accessed November 12, 2013, http://www. tshaonline.org/handbook/online/articles/rnr05

[xxxiii] W.W. Follett, 1898, Rio Grande Waters, Equitable Distribution of Waters of the Rio Grande: Message of the President of the United States. 55th Congress, Second Session, *U.S. Senate document 229*, U.S. Government Printing Office, Washington. Quoted in Neal Ackerly, "Water Challenges on the Lower Rio Grande." In Water Resource Research Institute Proceedings 1998. New Mexico State University, Las Cruces, NM. Accessed 11/28/2013. http://wrri.nmsu.edu/ publish/watcon/proc43/ackerly.pdf

# Part III

## . . . and the Valley Comes to the U.S.

# Guadalupe Hidalgo

With the end of the War with Mexico , in 1848, the U.S. had completely conquered that country. President Polk at one point even considered annexing the whole of it and there was a movement among some congressional members in this direction, but it was agreed in the end that the U.S. would be granted what would become the states of California, New Mexico, Arizona, Utah, Nevada, and parts of Wyoming, Colorado, Kansas and Oklahoma -- lands together referred to as the Mexican Cession. If the loss of Texas is included in this as well (both Texas proper and the disputed lands of eastern New Mexico), Mexico had ceded about 55% of the territory it controlled only a few years earlier. Conversely, the United States, in adding Texas and the Mexican Cession, increased its territory dramatically—today, this land composes slightly more than one quarter of the entire area of the country. (An interesting aside—during the Arab oil embargo of 1976, the U.S. asked Mexico for preferential oil purchases. Their response—"Remember the Treaty of Guadalupe Hidalgo.")

The agreement that would cement this massive transfer of land was called the Treaty of Guadalupe Hidalgo, after the town where it was signed and which has since been incorporated into Mexico City. The treaty was negotiated on behalf of the U.S. by a man named Nicholas Trist, in whom President Polk lost faith at one point and tried to recall to Washington. Trist ignored the recall order and finished his business in Mexico City where the treaty was signed on the 2nd of February, 1848. Under the treaty terms, Mexico received 15 million dollars plus the payment of its debts to U.S. citizens. Polk was furious but could do nothing about it at that point.

And it wasn't too long after the signing that big problems with the treaty began to arise, having to do with exactly where Mexico ended and this new part of the United States began. The treaty called for the western boundary between New Mexico and Mexico to start eight miles north of El Paso at the Rio Grande. The precise location was to be determined by surveyors from both countries. These surveys would take seven years to complete and would lead not only to errors but also disagreements driven by the national interests on both sides.

The largest issue that came to light though was the fact that the map used in the original negotiations, known as the Disturnell map, turned out to be wrong. Disturnell placed El Paso, by some estimates, as much as 42 miles north of its actual location.[xxxiv] Other sources have the mistaken location of El Paso slightly less distant from true, at around 30 miles. The effect was that, if that map were used to enforce the terms of the Treaty, much of the Mesilla Valley as well as valuable mines to the west at Santa Rita would be in Mexico.

However, in the fairly small window of time between the signing of Guadalupe Hidalgo in 1848 and the onset of the official surveying in late 1850, much would change and develop in the area around the Rio Grande south of Doña Ana. The effect of the surveying and the mistaken Disturnell map would have many repercussions.

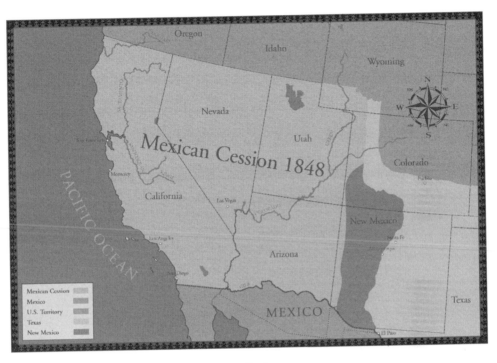

Tu Media Group

The Mexican Cession, which ended at the Rio Grande, and claimed land of Texas including the disputed territories of eastern New Mexico, Colorado, Oklahoma and Kansas (pink). The part outlined at the bottom was the disputed area, initially included as part of Mexico but soon to be re-negotiated.

# The Creation of Las Cruces and the First Forays Across the River

Almost immediately after Guadalupe Hidalgo made New Mexico an American territory, things changed in the town of Doña Ana. A U.S. Military outpost was established there to help protect against Indian raids. Initially it consisted of 87 men led by Lieutenant Delos B. Sackett. Other U.S. citizens were moving into the area too, looking for land. The problem was that, while there was plenty of land around Doña Ana, not much of it was irrigated and farmable. Also, in spite of the military presence, the Indian raids grew worse again, making farming very difficult. Livestock was stolen and settlers killed.

Additionally, some of the newcomers were Texans still claiming that this territory east of the river was part of their state, and, although Guadalupe Hidalgo guaranteed that any previous settlers could keep their land, the Texans began either taking over homesteads outright or laying claims.

In any case, in early 1849 a group of settlers established a camp to the south began to dig a new acequia from the river. Later that year, the Prefect or *Alcalde* of Doña Ana, asked Lt. Sackett to survey a new town site near the end of the acequia. After drawing lots from new settlers, Lt. Delos Bennett Sackett laid out an 84-block grid using rawhide ropes. The blocks were divided into quarter lots, and twenty eight of them (112 lots) were soon settled. This would become the Mesquite neighborhood in the city of Las Cruces, which still of course stands today.

The accepted wisdom regarding the naming of Las Cruces—often repeated in official histories as well as casual accountings—is that the name originated from an Apache massacre of about forty travelers from Taos, perhaps in 1830 or 1839 or 1840, near the future site of the town, and that the resulting "garden of crosses" became the town's namesake. There is however virtually no direct evidence of such an attack nor of one specific group of crosses on the town's site. (There would have been crosses all up and down the Camino Real.)

In fact, "Las Cruces" in old Spanish means The Crossing. The town was situated at an old crossing of roads that had existed since long before the Spanish arrived. The north-south trail along the river was crossed by one, running west from Florida to San Diego, that crossed the Organ Mountains and then followed the Alameda Arroyo down into the valley to a crossing at the river. Later, of course, the north-south route became the Camino Real and the east-west trail led to the town of Picacho, a well-used resting or gathering place, on the far side of the river, and then across to Arizona (largely the route that the wagon trains would later follow, once they were across the river). This crossroads was situated at the location of today's three crosses—in the vicinity of Alameda Avenue where it comes into Doña Ana Road.

As early as 1844, even before the founding of Las Cruces, the Tewa Pueblo Indians of Guadalupe, mentioned above, began to move back into the Mesilla Valley from Texas, the "former home of their Manso ancestors."[xxxv] The tribe began to hold dances in front of St. Genevieve's Catholic Church but, because of various controversies, eventually (in 1910) moved the ceremony to the small settlement of Tortugas, at the southern edge of Las Cruces. Some families moved to Tortugas but "most . . . continued to live in southeast Las Cruces in an area known as "Las Liebres."[xxxvi] The annual ceremonies continue in Tortugas to this day.

# Mesilla Comes Alive

Also in 1849 a few hardy campers began to cross the river and settle on the little plateau overlooking the river from the west, the same plateau where Oñate had camped hundreds of years before—the place he called the *Trenquel de la Mesilla*. There were no acequias dug yet, and the real influx would not begin for another year, in the spring of 1850, so life would have been rough at best. Still, according to the National Register of Historic Places of the U.S. Department of the Interior, a two-room jacal was built on what would become the Mesilla Plaza in 1849 -- the beginnings of what would become today's Double Eagle Restaurant.

It is commonly believed, and noted in many histories of this area and this time, that the town of Mesilla was created because the Mexican settlers of Doña Ana wanted to live in Mexico, not the U.S. After the Treaty of Guadalupe Hidalgo, Doña Ana, lying east of the river, was clearly in the U.S. now (and possibly even in Texas, if that new state's claims were to be accepted). The theory is that, because of the mistakes in the Disturnell map and of the surveyors, the plateau where Mesilla would be founded now lay in Mexico, that is, west of the river and below the mistaken border. However, that border was not established officially until late in 1850, and it is not in fact entirely clear whether, before that, the area west of the Rio Grande and north of the traditional border extending west of El Paso was considered by the U.S. and Mexico to be U.S. territory or not.

In 1849, a letter to the governor of Chihuahua asks for clarification on exactly where "La Mecia" is located so that settlers " . . . may move their people, and they may know under what country's law they must make their petition."[xxxvii] Research into the earliest title claims in Mesilla shows that, "In March of 1850, both Mexico and the United States assume that Mesilla is part of the new United States territory of New Mexico, since it had always been part of New Mexico."[xxxviii]

However, the U.S. Boundary Commissioner appointed to sort out the surveying situation, John Russell Bartlett, wrote that after the war:

> . . . the Mexican population occupying the eastern bank of the Rio Grand in Texas and New Mexico were greatly annoyed by the encroachments of the Americans, and by their determined efforts to despoil them of their landed property. This was done by the latter either settling among them, or in some instances forcibly occupying their dwellings and cultivated spots. In most cases, however, it was done by putting "Texas head-right" on their property . . . [w]ith these land certificates . . . many Americans flocked to the valley of the Rio Grande, and in repeated instances, located them on the property which for a century had been in the quiet possession of the descendants of the old Spanish colonists.[xxxix]

The U.S. government of course took issue with these new land claims, and when Texas sent troops to enforce its claims, federal troops were sent as well to protect the rights of the Mexican settlers. In the end, after the Compromise of 1850, Texas relinquished its claim, but the combined stresses had already apparently proved too much for many settlers, who moved across the river to Mesilla.[xl]

Other research indicates that settlers were coming into Mesilla as early as 1849, and that most of them were not new Americans nor were they from Doña Ana. "In the summer of 1849    . . . colonists had begun to arrive in the area of La Mesilla from northern New Mexico and from the Pass—ethnically different Indian, mestizo, Spaniard—all of them Mexican citizens."[xli]

In any case, what is known for sure is that on March 1 of 1850 a man named Don Rafael Ruelas, who had previously led followers from a grant near El Paso to Doña Ana[xlii], and believing (at least according to Bartlett) that he was returning from Doña Ana to Mexican territory, led a group "most of whom had been domiciled at Doña Ana [to abandon] their homes on account of their many grievances, and [move] to the lands known as the Mesilla, where they established themselves." Bartlett goes on to say that, "More than half the population of Doña Ana removed to Mesilla within a year."[xliii] The 1850 census counted about 700 people in Mesilla.

But it is also clear that Mesilla was not only populated originally by disgruntled Mexicans from Doña Ana. Both Americans and Mexicans had settled there from the first, including a man named Thomas Bull who testified that he first came to the area of Doña Ana as a clerk under Doniphan, and later that he, "moved to Mesilla in March or April of 1851 when it was still considered part of the United States. He also [said] that the town site was surveyed at that time and divided into 160-acre lots, measuring 960 by 960 varas."[xliv]

And there were apparently other Americans as well. "Among the first Americans to establish themselves on the Mesilla side of the river was Louis William Geck, a private honorably discharged at Doña Ana from Company H, First Regiment United States Dragoons. Don Luis, as he came to be known, was born in Poland."[xlv] Other former-soldiers who came down with Doniphan settled in the area as well—from Doña Ana to Las Cruces to Mesilla.

Bartlett, however, writing of these earliest years in Mesilla, said that "Very few Americans ever settled there—in fact, none but traders, and it is probably that there never were twenty altogether."

In any case, Mesilla would grow after this while Doña Ana and Las Cruces remained very small towns of only a few hundred people each. In spite of this, Las Cruces would become for the time being the Doña Ana county seat simply by virtue of the fact that it would remain in the U.S., while for Mesilla that would not be the case.

# Mesilla Moves to Mexico

By late in the year of 1850, Boundary Commissioner Bartlett, who had been appointed the previous year to step in and straighten out the confusion engendered by the faulty Disturnell map, came to a somewhat startling conclusion about which country Mesilla lay within. His Mexican counterpart, General Pedro García Conde, argued that, based on latitude and longitude in the original map, the border should be located some 34 miles north and 130 miles east of where Bartlett originally thought it should be. The men struck a deal, agreeing that Mexico would keep the Mesilla Valley, or at least part of it, and the U.S. would hold the Santa Rita mines, near Silver City. The line, based on what became know as the Bartlett-Conde Compromise, was placed just north of Las Cruces, heading westward from the Rio Grande for a distance before cutting north to the Gila River and westward along it from there, passing well north of modern day Tucson. Later Bartlett's supervisor, who had been sick at the time of the compromise, would refuse to sign the agreement, stating that Bartlett was duped.[xlvi] Still, at least for the time being, the Bartlett-García Conde Line was accepted and Mesilla, since it lay to the west of the river and slightly to the south, was now officially in Mexico.

In April of 1851, upon confirmation that the Conde-Bartlett compromise placed Mesilla in Mexico, the citizens fired cannons and had a grand ball to celebrate. Thomas Bull, the former U.S. army clerk, however was not pleased. In his testimony he stated that, "as soon as he learned that Mesilla was part of Mexico, he moved to Las Cruces, because he wanted to be in the United States."[xlvii]

The Mexican government immediately passed the Colonization Act of May 22, 1851, and began to issue grants in this new area of settlement under the auspices of Father Ramon Ortiz, "the *cura* at Paso del Norte . . . "[xlviii] Ortiz would become the first commissioner of Mesilla, and would name Don Rafael Ruelas the first *alcalde*, or magistrate.[xlix] John Russell Bartlett himself described the new community that same year—"It consists of mud, or chiefly of stick houses, and has been settled within two years by Mexicans who have abandoned their residences on our side of the river . . . ."[l] In August of that year of 1851, Ortiz issued the first deed in Mesilla to Antonio Uribes and a few months later a census showed over 1200 people living there.[li] New families each received a quarter of a grid block. In early 1852, Ortiz would issue the Mesilla Civil Colony Grant.

Father Ortiz also founded the San Albino church, and the first permanent priest of San Albino, Bernardino Hinojos, was appointed in 1852. It was named, in the manner of such churches then, after the first acequia that came into Mesilla, on San Albino day. The common conception of these earliest years of San Albino are that services were held in a rectory or some other mud building on the south side of the plaza, across from where the church now stands. "The settlers soon established a central plaza which included a Catholic church on the south side of the plaza. Constructed of mud and logs, this primitive structure was named San Albino."[lii]

And Maude McFie in her 1903 thesis quotes the Hon. Horace Stephenson as having said, of Mesilla in 1853, "I do not think there were twelve houses in La Mesilla then. It was a very large heavily populated town, but the houses were all jacals; even the church was only a jacal, and was situated then on the east side of the Plaza, opposite from where it is now."[liii]

However, it is not clear what direct evidence supports the claim of such a structure on the south or east side of the square. There is no support in the official records.

> The most commonly suggested location for an "original" church is the block immediately south of the plaza, known as the Overland Stage block, but the property deeds fully account for the owners of that block with no sign of church ownership . . . There is also no evidence of the existing church block being purchased in the deed records . . . These arguments convince this author that the Mesilla church was always located on the block where it is now.[liv]

The first jacal mud San Albino Church, built in 1852, was replaced by a more permanent structure completed in 1857 at the north end of the Plaza. (This structure would be rebuilt in 1885, and again in 1908. See photos and captions near the end of section V for the progression of the church buildings).

A couple of interesting notes on Father Ortiz: when the Texas-Santa Fe expedition was captured by Mexican forces in 1840 and led south, as described above, they were, according to the memoir of George Kendall, in pretty bad shape when they reached El Paso. There they were taken care of, saved even, by none other than Father Ramon Ortiz. Some years later, Ortiz was captured by Doniphan when he occupied El Paso after the battle of Brazito and held for a time.[lv]

In 1853, Ortiz was replaced as commissioner of Mesilla by Guadalupe Miranda. Miranda then separated the Mesilla Civil Colony Grant into two separate grants—the Santo Tomás de Iturbide Grant and the Picacho Grant to the north.[lvi] By 1854, a military census listed a population in Mesilla of more than 3,000, compared with only 600 in Las Cruces.

So it was, in any case, that the town of Mesilla was born fairly abruptly—perhaps so that many of its residents could escape the US and return to Mexico. Sadly for them, in that case, this situation would only last a couple of more years.

For another force was coming to bear on the area—the need for reliable efficient transportation. As it was, goods headed west could only proceed beyond Paso del Norte by wagon. This situation would persist for some time, and would actually benefit Mesilla greatly, but there was already a strong sense that a railroad, sooner or later, would eventually need to come through the area, connecting the south and Texas with the new southwest and California. And that sense doomed the Bartlett-García Conde agreement as to where the US now ended and Mexico began.

Tu Media Group

This map is adapted from one that appeared in the June 4, 1853, edition of the *Illustrated News* (NY), showing the disputed territory south of the tentative border established just south of Las Cruces ("Boundary claimed by Mexico"). Note the differences in the "True position of El Paso" and the "Erroneous position of El Paso" which locates it just south of the new settlement of Mesilla.

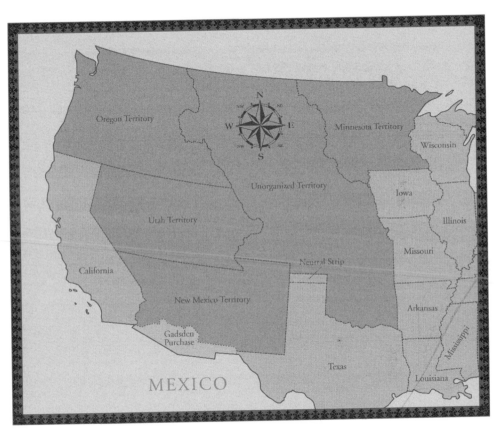

Tu Media Group

A map of the United States in the early 1850s, after organization of the Mexican Cession but before the Gadsden Purchase. The Disputed Territory that would be the focus of Gadsden is in pink.

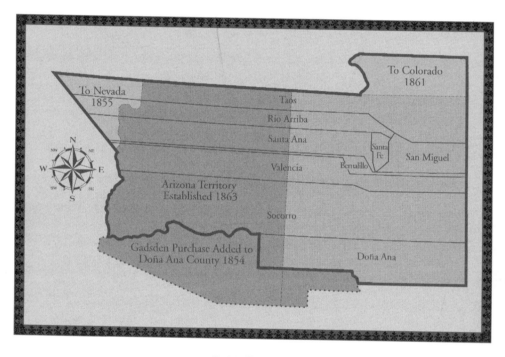

Tu Media Group

Map from around 1852 showing the original Doña Ana county, before the Gadsden purchase, the territory of which was then added on to Doña Ana County, extending it clear to the California border.

# A Rail's Future Gleam—the Dream Behind the Gadsden Purchase

As one can see from the 1853 newspaper map on page 76, the area between Las Cruces and El Paso and regions west was not referred to as Mexico but the Disputed Territory. The agreement between Bartlett and García Conde never sat well with many, and now things were changing again in the short time after it was signed.

After the discovery of gold at Sutter's Mill in 1849 and the granting of statehood to California in 1850, a great and almost immediate migration began of eastern Americans and foreigners to this new land. Something like 300,000 people would arrive in the next five years. It was becoming more and more apparent that railroads crossing the country were needed, and one of the primes routes seemed to be across southern New Mexico and Arizona (as opposed to one crossing the more mountainous middle of the territories). Though it would be some decades before this route was finally realized, its anticipation was a big part of the impetus to settle the territorial dispute with Mexico.

In 1852 Franklin Pierce was elected president, the Democrats were taking over from the Whigs, and with that change came many others. The new Secretary of War was a Mexican war General, veteran and Mississippi Senator named Jefferson Davis. At Davis' urging, James Gadsden was appointed foreign minister to Mexico. This appointment would have a direct bearing on the ultimate fate of the Disputed Territory, for Gadsden was himself both a southerner and a staunch advocate of slavery as well as a railroad man, having headed the South Carolina Railroad from 1840-1850. His interest therefore was not only in establishing a trans-continental rail line but specifically one that linked the slave states directly with California. "To expand slavery and secure it against North opposition, Gadsden looked to the west. He hoped to unite it with the South, partly by taking slaves west and partly through an imaginative railroad system," and he, " . . . wanted to establish a slaveholding colony in southern California that would produce rice, cotton, and sugar . . ." and to, " . . . [build] a southern railroad to the gold country, starting either from Red River or from San Antonio."[lvii] Originally, Gadsden envisioned this rail running across north Texas and the middle of the southwestern territories, but he later decided that the most direct and feasible route was across the extreme southwestern edge of the U.S. The problem was that, under the Bartlett-García Conde Compromise, that edge still lay in Mexico.

Another wrinkle was that, in 1852, the governor of the New Mexico territory, William Carr Lane, led a small expedition south from Santa Fe to take control of the entire Mesilla Valley, this notwithstanding the fact that he had almost no military support. This led to the Mexicans massing troops on the border at Paso, escalating tensions and creating the need for some kind of U.S. response. Almost none came, at least militarily, but for a short time "It appeared as though the Battle of Brazito might have a sequel in the Mesilla Valley."[lviii] Lane was discredited and accused of having badly muddied the situation. A new governor was appointed. And now feathers, starting with those of Santa Anna (who had yet again become the Mexican dictator), had to be smoothed.

The man to do the smoothing was James Gadsden. At first, the approach Gadsden took was just that—to placate. Any demands for the immediate transfer of land, as Governor Lane had insisted, were put on hold. Things would stay as they were until negotiations had been completed. Gadsden's real goal of course was to buy the land. The main rationale for this (and the only one Gadsden really cared about) was to secure a route for a southern transcontinental railroad. The land across the middle of New Mexico and Arizona was mountainous, but that along the southern border, if it could be secured, was flat and open most of the way.

Still, President Pierce had by then set his sights higher, which led to a somewhat convoluted and dragged out negotiation. Per Pierce's instructions, Gadsden's first offer was $50 million for a much larger portion of northern Mexico than the Disputed Territory including all of Baja, California. That was rejected. The second offer of $35 million was for land adjoining the Arizona and California borders including the northern part of the Gulf of California, thus providing Arizona with a seaport. That was not accepted either. Subsequent offers, each for progressively smaller amounts of land, were for $30 million and then $20 million. Gadsden didn't really care about the reductions in territory, but he would give no sway on what was required for the railroad and he left no doubt that he would get it, one way or another. He said, "The projected railroad from New York to California must be built by way of the Mesilla Valley because there is no other feasible route . . . The valley must belong to the United States by an indemnity, or we will take it."[lix] Santa Anna, who was grappling with a crippling national debt, had to sell something. Spurred by that along with Gadsden's threat, President Santa Anna agreed to let the Disputed Territories go for $15 million.[lx]

In 1854 the U S Congress ratified the Gadsden Treaty or *Tratado de Mesilla*, though only after much fighting, with a reduction in the amount of land from nearly 40 thousand square miles to less than 30, and a reduction of the purchase price to $10 million. President Polk signed on June 9. Thus, on November 16, 1854, in "a public ceremony on the plaza," Mesilla and 29,670 square miles of land were annexed into Doña Ana County and thus Mesilla once again became part of the United States.[lxi]

The border set then with Mexico is the one that still exists today.

In the Name of Almighty God.

The Republic of Mexico and the United States of America desiring to remove every cause of disagreement, which might interfere in any manner with the better friendship and intercourse between the two countries; and especially, in respect to the true limits which should be established, when notwithstanding what was covenanted in the Treaty of Guadalupe Hidalgo in the year 1848, opposite interpretations have been urged, — which might give occasion to questions of serious moment: to avoid these, and to strengthen and more firmly maintain the peace, which happily prevails between the two Republics, the President

The first and last pages of the English version of the Gadsden Treaty as negotiated December, 1853.

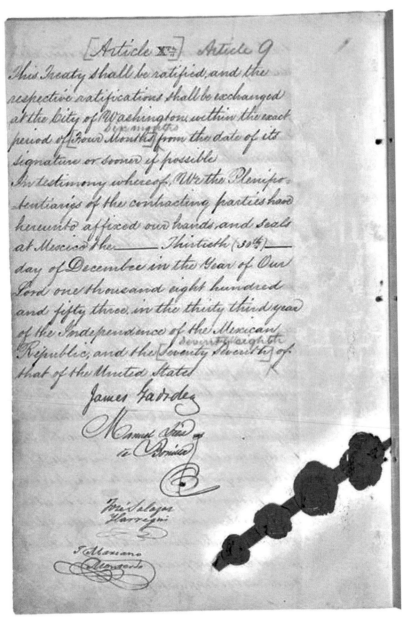

[Article X~~] Article 9

This Treaty shall be ratified, and the respective ratifications shall be exchanged at the City of Washington, within the exact period of ~~Four Months~~ six months from the date of its signature or sooner if possible.

In testimony whereof, We the Plenipotentiaries of the contracting parties have hereunto affixed our hands and seals at Mexico the ___ Thirtieth (30th) ___ day of December in the Year of Our Lord one thousand eight hundred and fifty three, in the thirty third year of the Independence of the Mexican Republic, and the ~~Seventy~~ seventy eighth of that of the United States.

James Gadsden

Manuel Diez de Bonilla

Jose Salazar Ylarregui

J. Mariano Monterde

General Records of the U.S. Government, Record Group 11;
National Archives Building, Washington DC

83

1953 U.S. Postal Stamp commemorating the 100th anniversary
of the Gadsen Purchase.

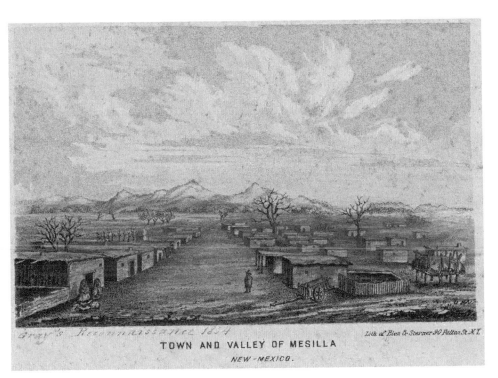

Valley and Town of Mesilla, New Mexico," 1854; Image No. 03390024; Courtesy of New Mexico
State University Archives and Special Collections

Carl Schuchard lithograph of Mesilla, 1854.

# The Guard and the Military

With the relocation of the southwestern territories into the U.S. after Guadalupe Hidalgo, and then the 1849 gold rush, the area grew quickly in importance. More specifically, the potentially fertile Mesilla Valley and the new town of Mesilla itself did too, both as a corridor and as a destination. The California Road, which ran from Arkansas to the gold fields in the west, passed from El Paso directly through Mesilla and on to Tucson. The real problem, even as the situation leading up to Gadsden was resolving itself, was still and ever the Indians—the Comanches and the Apaches. Bartlett the surveyor noted the problem in his writings and, in 1853, an Army inspector named Mansfield commented that the vast potential of the area would never be realized as long as "the Apaches roamed freely about the countryside and swooped down upon the settlements at their leisure."[lxii]

One source of attempted redress locally was the establishment of the Mesilla Guard, a militia group composed of household members from the community. This group tried to ward off Indian attacks but also retaliated, often viciously and against particular natives who were guilty of nothing but being in the wrong place at the wrong time. So tensions were heightened more between the natives and the settlers.

Another more important attempt to deal with the situation was the establishment of military installations along the trail. One of these, Fort Fillmore, was built in 1851 only a few miles south of Mesilla. Its remains today lie within the huge Salopek orchards you pass through on I-10 just south of its junction with I-25, in the pecan trees to the west. Fillmore was important to Mesilla not only as a source of protection against the Indians but also as a purchaser of supplies. Before Gadsden settled the issue of Mesilla's place in the U.S., some of the merchants and freighters who had set up there moved back across the river to Las Cruces, but with Mesilla's return in 1854, the village, being closer to the fort than either Las Cruces or Doña Ana, became the supply center for the garrisoned troops, providing entertainment, food, hay and building materials. In addition, La Mesilla was to become a shipping and travel hub, and much larger than Las Cruces, with more businesses that offered more goods and services. In 1855 when the town became again part of Doña Ana County, the court house and with it the county seat were transferred to Mesilla from little Las Cruces. With the gold and silver mining in the area, farming, ranching and the town's location directly on the main southern east-west corridor, Mesilla was quickly evolving into the major trading center of southern New Mexico.

# Before The Rail, The Stage—
# The Jackass and the
# Butterfield Overland

Mail arrived every so often in Mesilla from the bags of men who rode horses on a route between San Antonio and Santa Fe. Wagon trains of various sorts passed through, bringing or taking supplies and ore and people. But there was a clear need for the establishment of a major organized transcontinental route from the east to California. Although a rail cutting across the desert had been envisioned, it would not become reality for some years. The first transcontinental line crossing the U.S. would be completed well to the north, across northern Nevada and Utah, in 1869. The Southern Transcontinental line, as it was known, would not be completed until 1882. But for those intervening years, a lot of goods and people, as well as the U.S. Mail, needed to move in both directions. And what moved were wagons.

One problem with wagons of course is that they are not good in heavy snow or in mountains. The advantage of a route that crossed the southernmost edge of the western U.S., even though it was much longer than a line farther north, was that it was flat and could be used year round. The drawback of course was that it crossed a series of deserts, but it was still, at least according to Aaron Brown, the U.S. Postmaster General at the time, the most efficient way to go.

Other small lines existed but the first major one was the San Antonio-San Diego Mail Line, established by a man named James Birch, the head of the California Stage Company. It was also called Jackass Mail because its wagons were pulled most often by mules rather than horses. Sometimes the passengers would even have to walk to relieve the balky animals.[lxiii] One significance of the Jackass Mail was that it had a regular stop in Mesilla—the first time the town was not an offshoot of a different line. Birch, however, drowned in a sea accident at the time of the very first run of the line, and so it didn't last long, running into the early 1860s but only at the eastern and western ends of the original route.

In the next year, 1858, John Warren Butterfield contracted with the Post Office to establish the Butterfield-Overland Line. In addition to mail, he made a significant part of the business transporting passengers. Though it too would have a limited run, also lasting only into the early 1860s when it was taken over by Well Fargo, the Butterfield-Overland lives on in history. One of the innovations of the endeavor was the substitution, on the western part of the route (basically west of El Paso), of a lighter type of vehicle sometimes called a Celerity wagon for the typical heavy coaches of the day. The problem the Jackass Mail and the early runs of the Butterfield had was that the iconic Concord coaches that we associate with the old west were just too heavy for the sandy routes across New Mexico and Arizona. The Celerity-type wagon was more upright with open sides covered only by curtains, and a cloth roof, and a lighter suspension system, thus reducing its weight dramatically. It also had a wider wheelbase to stabilize it. Interestingly, though, while the Celerity wagon has passed down through time as the savior of these Western routes, there was not actually a wagon manufactured under the name Celerity. Celerity, rather, "was a vernacular term, or common parlance term, used by many writers and diarists to describe a type of stage coach or stage wagon. We have [no reliable information] about it, except verbal descriptions. Most of the illustrations are imaginative, but do try and capture the image. The problem is that it is incomplete."[lxiv]

Regardless, these treks across the country were adventures, to say the least. Indian attacks, weather, and bad terrain took their toll. The total length of the journey was around 2800 miles and took an average of 21 days.[lxv] Maude McFie tells us that, "The fare from start to finish was $150.00, meals being provided by the company at stations, and forty pounds of baggage was allowed. At each station a guard of six or seven men (at $75.00 and board per month) was kept to look out for relays of horses . . . This was of immediate benefit to the valley, not only in transporting outsiders and mail, but because the Company purchases all its provisions from the villagers, thus setting in circulation plenty of money. This was a tri-weekly line."[lxvi]

The block directly south of the Plaza in Mesilla became the Overland Stage block—the area where now Nambe and El Patio Bar reside and the entire block south of along Calle Principal. The fourth and fifth lots down, including the space where Vintage Wines is now, were the location of the Southern Overland Mail and Express Company itself.[lxvii]

Many of the buildings on and around the Plaza date back to this early time, but that's not the case with the stage area. The buildings right on the Plaza, that now house the front part of El Patio and Nambe, are not original. The structures behind them however are. According the National Register of Historic Places, the building behind El Patio housed a saloon and billiard room, and the building behind (south of) that at one time housed the offices of the Jackass Mail.

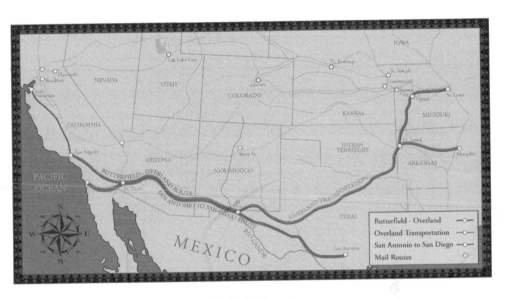

Tu Media Group

San Antonio to San Diego (Jackass) route in 1857, the Butterfield-Overland Route from St. Louis and Memphis to San Francisco, and the San Antonio to San Diego (a.k.a. The Jackass Line).

Frank Leslie's Illustrated Newspaper, October 23, 1858.

A version of a Celerity-type wagon.[lxviii]

xxxiv Michael Dear, "Monuments, Manifest Destiny, and Mexico," *Prologue Magazine*, 37, no. 2 (2005), http://www.archives.gov/publications/prologue/2005/summer/mexico-1.html (accessed November 15, 2013)

xxxv Torres, unpublished

xxxvi Torres, unpublished

xxxvii David G. Thomas, "La Posta: From the Founding of Mesilla to Corn Exchange Hotel to Billy the Kid Museum to Famous Landmarks." (Las Cruces, NM: Doc45 Publishing, 2014), 8

xxxviii Thomas, *La Posta*, 8

xxxix John Russell Bartlett. "Explorations and Incidents in Texas, New Mexico, California, Sonora and Chihuahua -- Volume II." (New York, NY: D. Appleton & Co., 1855), accessed 11-12/2013, http://www.biodiversitylibrary.org/ia/mobot31753000248002#page/5/mode/1up

xl Kiser, *Turmoil*, 40

xli Mary Daniels Taylor, "A Place as Wild as the West Ever Was." (Las Cruces, NM: New Mexico State University Museum, 2004), 25

xlii Thomas, *La Posta*, 30

xliii Bartlett, *Explorations*

xliv Thomas, *La Posta*, 8-9

xlv Taylor, *A Place*, 30

xlvi Martin Donell Kohout, "BARTLETT-GARCIA CONDE COMPROMISE," *Handbook of Texas Online*, published by the Texas State Historical Association. (http://www.tshaonline.org/handbook/online/articles/nbb02), accessed November 15, 2013

xlvii Thomas, *La Posta*, 9

xlviii Kiser, *Turmoil*, 39

xlix Thomas, *La Posta*, 30

l Kiser, *Turmoil*, 40

li Thomas, *La Posta*, 14

lii Basilica of San Albino, "Basilica History -- Establishment of La Mesilla and San Albino." Research based on pamphlet by Mary Daniels Taylor called "History of San Albino on the Plaza." Accessed December 12, 2013. http://www.sanalbino.org/1ChHist.html

liii McFie, *History*, 21

liv Thomas, *La Posta*, 34-35

lv Thomas, *La Posta*, 31

lvi Damico, Denise. NewMexicoHistory.org, "Mesilla Civil Colony Grant." Accessed December 11, 2013. http://newmexicohistory.org/places/mesilla-civil-colony-grant.

lvii Richards, Leonard, "The California Gold Rush and the Coming of the Civil War," (New York, NY: Knopf, 2007), 125-126

lviii Kiser, *Turmoil*, 74

lix Richards, *Gold Rush*, 150-152

lx ibid, *150-152*

lxi Thomas, *La Posta*, 12

[lxii] Kiser, *Turmoil*, 98

[lxiii] Historian, "Overland Mail to California in the 1850s," United States Postal Service, August 2010, http://about.usps.com/who-we-are/postal-history/overland-mail.htm

[lxiv] Ken Wheeling, unpublished letter, April 4, 2014

[lxv] Historian, *Overland*

[lxvi] McFie, *History*, 33

[lxvii] Thomas, *La Posta*, 40

[lxviii] Frank Leslie's Illustrated Newspaper, October 23, 1858.

# Part IV

## War and Its Violent Aftermath

# The Separatists and the Prelude to War

While the majority of citizens in Mesilla (by and large former Mexicans) had no particular stake in the impending U.S. Civil War, a smaller group of Caucasian businessmen, mostly from Texas, did. These men were pro-slavery and considered themselves a part of the American south. There was actually at that time another plaza in Mesilla, called the Gran Plaza, which would have been where the San Andres High School is now, three blocks east of the main plaza. This was created by these businessmen, " . . . neat town blocks laid out ready for new businesses and new homes of Southern sympathizers. Settling in this Plaza was a nucleus of Missourians, Kansans, and Texans with Anglo wives and of the Protestant faith."[lxix]

There was in fact a mock presidential election held in Mesilla in 1860. Though it had no official bearing, it was reported as far away as San Francisco and went overwhelming against Lincoln—who received only 5 votes. The same was true to the south, in El Paso.[lxx] If the election held no real consequence, however, subsequent conventions of landowners from Mesilla and towns farther west did. The issue of these conventions was to "subscribe to the Confederacy."[lxxi] These flames were fanned hotly by the Mesilla *Times*, an important influencer of opinion both locally and across the southwest.

Another festering issue, affected directly by the impending national split, was the refusal of U.S. Congress to create an official Arizona Territory out of fear that any state resulting from that declaration would be slave-holding. Compounding this for Mesilla and Arizona residents was the fact that the government's contract with the Butterfield-Overland Company was revoked in 1861, further isolating settlers and "demonstrat[ing] to the people [in the territory] that they were of minimal importance in the eyes of the United States Government."[lxxii]

The truth was that the corridor across New Mexico and Arizona led directly to California and the fear was that the influence of the settlers here would bleed over into that state which had, to the surprise of many, voted for Lincoln. In addition to fears of California turning pro-slavery, perhaps an even more important aspect were the gold fields—the Confederacy would see these and the ports as a way of financing itself, and the war. The Union knew that the gold there lay behind the credit it would need to prosecute the war itself. Control of this corridor across New Mexico and Arizona then became a very important issue in the lead up to war.

In March of 1861, conventions were held in Mesilla and then in Tucson, with representatives from 14 towns in the two vicinities. The two together established a Territory of Arizona and declared its sympathies to lie with the Confederacy. They also, although they adopted the laws of New Mexico, rejected the authority of the government of the New Mexico territory as well. [lxxiii] Although the Confederacy itself didn't immediately recognize it as a new Territory (it would shortly, by the end of 1861), a new, if temporary, territory now existed that became a de facto state of the Confederacy. It would last for a couple of years, until 1863, when Lincoln would sign the Arizona Organic Act that created modern-day Arizona as we know it. But before that, the heat of the great war itself would find its way directly into the heart of La Mesilla.

There is first, though, a larger picture to be noted. Remember that Jefferson Davis himself, as of early 1861 the president of the Confederacy, was really the driving force behind the Gadsden Purchase when he served as Secretary of War in the 1850s. Add to this the fact that, in the years preceding the war, a virtual Who's Who of future confederate leaders served time in the New Mexico Territory, including Longstreet, Reynolds, and Ewell.[lxxiv] It is also believed that Davis had designs not only on taking over California but further parts of Mexico as well, as a way of giving the Confederacy more land and also access to more ports.

After the April, 1861, convention that established
the Confederate Territory of Arizona, comprising the southern halves of the
two original territories, the Southern-sympathizing Mesilla Times began
printing its location as Mesilla, Arizona.

# The Confederacy Invades the "North"—via Mesilla

The tension in the southern Mesilla Valley is signified by the simple distance—some five miles—that lay between the secessionists and slave-trade supporters who ran Mesilla and the federal troops garrisoned at Fort Fillmore under the recently arrived Major Isaac Lynde. In June of 1861 someone in Mesilla ". . . wrote to President Davis advocating an invasion of New Mexico . . ." [lxxv] It's doubtful that this letter had much of an effect on Davis other than to perhaps further convince him that an invasion would be welcomed by the residents (at least the white land owners and the editors of the Mesilla *Times*—whether the Mexican-descended locals cared much for the idea of a Confederate invasion is a far more questionable proposition). General Henry Sibley, who had been a federal officer in Arizona before resigning to join the Confederacy, knew the territory and advocated its taking by the South as well. Clearly the catalyst that would ignite the situation in Mesilla derived from the simple fact that, for the South to realize its designs on California and northern Mexico, it had to first kick the Union forces out of New Mexico—southern New Mexico was the gatekeeper that would allow access to the rest of the southwest.

In July, 1861, Confederate lieutenant John Baylor, leading a somewhat scruffy outfit, was sent west from San Antonio to El Paso. "Nearly the entire invading rebel force was poorly armed with obsolete rifles and muskets, and were inadequately clothed and equipped for the journey through the desert."[lxxvi] Their arrival in El Paso was no secret, nor was the march north along the Rio Grande they began in July of that year, though it hardly mattered given the sorry state of the Union forces at Fort Fillmore—a fortress built to house Indian fighters, not to defend against artillery attacks. Some hold that Baylor headed north toward Fillmore and Mesilla to preclude an expected attack by Lynde's forces, others that the trek north was simply the next step in the planned takeover of New Mexico. The plan was to attack Fillmore, unprepared as it was, and capture the Union forces before they could retreat (which seemed to be their primary defensive plan anyway). Baylor's forces arrived on July 24 and, "by the evening of this date they . . . encamped within 600 yards of the outposts at Fort Fillmore."[lxxvii] This was, by the way, the first major invasion of "northern" territory by the south in the entire war. The problem was that an informer and Union sympathizer had slipped out ahead and warned Lynde of the impending attack. Their surprise ruined, Baylor's force continued the next day on to Mesilla where they were "received with every manifestation of joy . . ."[lxxviii]

Later that same day, July 25, Lynde's forces marched from the fort to Mesilla, and again, if surprise was the intention, it was a failure. The Confederate troops saw the dust of Lynde's forces from some distance away and were waiting. When Lynde sent envoys ahead to ask for surrender, Baylor returned word telling Lynde that if he wanted Mesilla, he'd have to take it. And so Lynde tried. The sand made moving the heavy artillery ineffective and when Baylor's forces commenced a kind of ambush, the battle turned quickly. Lynde would have approached Mesilla from the southeast, and so come into the outskirts somewhere around the today's intersection Avenida de Mesilla and University Avenue. In Lynde's own words:

> I moved the battery forward and fired two shells at long range, but they burst in the air short of the object. The command continued to advance slowly towards the outskirts of the town, while the battery, which had to be moved by hand, was working through the heavy sand. From a corn field and a house on the right, we received a heavy fire of musketry, wounding 2 officers and 4 men and killing 3 men. As night was coming on, and the fields and houses on both sides of the road were filled with men, and the howitzers useless, except as a field battery, owing to the difficulty of moving through the sand, I decided to withdraw my forces and return to my post[lxxix]

By the next morning, Lynde ordered the fort abandoned and burned, and attempted to move his men to Fort Stanton, quite a trek given that the fort lay nestled in the northern Sacramento Mountains well to the northeast of Ruidoso, and up the road from Lincoln. It seems that the men, though, before their retreat, filled their canteens (or had them filled) with whiskey instead of water. It may have been that the men simply wanted to get drunk, not realizing the arid hardships that lay ahead of them, but another possibility is that southern sympathizers within Lynde's command (and there were apparently many of them) actually sabotaged the water. "Given the fact that these officers were known to have anti-Union sentiments, it would not seem unlikely that many of them secretly *wanted* to surrender to Baylor. Thus it might not have been out of the question for the officers to allow the whiskey to be supplied to their troops just before embarking on the march to distant Fort Stanton."[lxxx]

Needless to say, their trek across the desert east of Las Cruces was not a success. Many men fell by the wayside and were gradually captured by Baylor's forces, who had learned of the retreat—both from the smoke of the burning fort and the clouds of dust raised by the retreating men—and given chase.[lxxxi] Lynde's immediate goal was to reach the springs at St. Augustin (today's Aguirre Springs), which Lynde himself and a few other officers accomplished. But, he later wrote, there was insufficient water to take back to all the men, and in any case they had all been overtaken at that point by Baylor's troops. Lynde surrendered, and so Fort Fillmore, and indeed southern New Mexico, was lost to the Confederacy—at least for the time being.

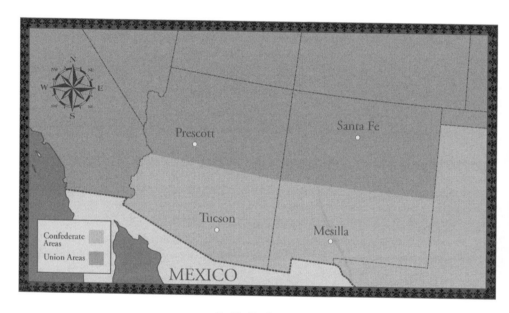

Tu Media Group

The state of New Mexico and Arizona in the early part of the Civil War. The green area in southern Arizona and New Mexico would be known as the Arizona Territory.

# Mesilla, Western Capital of the Confederacy

On August 1 of 1861, Lt. Baylor announced the creation of the Confederate Territory of Arizona. The territorial line ran just south of Socorro -- at the northern edge of the Jornada del Muerto. Mesilla would be its capital and Baylor himself would be governor. There is some evidence that his headquarters were housed in the Mease family compound, what is today the Double Eagle Restaurant on the east side of the Plaza.[lxxxii] Others claim differently, saying either across the plaza on the west side, or to the south—"A building was rented south of the Plaza to contain the territorial headquarters."[lxxxiii]

Baylor proved to be a harsh administrator. Dancing and theater performances were taxed; activities common to the culture, such as washing clothing in acequias, selling wood on the street, or butchering and selling animals were banned as well.[lxxxiv] The editor of the Mesilla *Times*, who had been so staunchly pro-South and pro-Slavery, began to write with displeasure about what was happening in Mesilla under Baylor. This tension was resolved quickly and brutally in December of that year when Baylor attacked the man in the street, resulting in his death two days later. Baylor also issued orders to invite Apaches to a peace ceremony and then ambush and slaughter them. The orders were never carried out but when word of them got back to Jefferson Davis, Baylor was relieved of his duties.

The next commander in Mesilla was General Henry Sibley. Sibley was a long time military man, his service dating back to the early 1840s when he was an Indian fighter in Florida. Before the Civil War he had been stationed in Arizona and New Mexico. When the war broke out in the spring of 1861, he resigned his commission to join the Confederacy. He would arrive very early in the next year (1862) in Mesilla with what he called The Army of New Mexico, consisting of about 3000 men. His task, like Baylor's, was to continue to gain ground for the Confederacy in the Southwest, especially farther north in New Mexico, and also to find sources of income—one possibility being gold mines in Colorado.

In December of 1861, while Baylor was still acting as governor and before Sibley entered New Mexico (he was holding at Fort Bliss), Sibley tried to convince the citizens, both Mexican and non, that joining the Confederacy would be good for them all. He even went so far as to have printed a proclamation to be distributed throughout the territory, although most copies seem to have been confiscated before they were widely read.[lxxxv] In the new year of 1862, Sibley would move his forces up the river to Fort Thorn (near present-day Hatch). Meanwhile, General Edward Canby, the leading Union officer in the New Mexico territory, had moved his forces as far south as Fort Craig, midway between Socorro and present-day Truth or Consequences (just south of the Bosque del Apache), roughly at the border between the Confederate Territory of Arizona and the non-Confederate northern territory of New Mexico. The forces of these two men, Sibley and Canby, along with other Union forces from farther north, were to decide the fate of the New Mexico and Arizona territories for the balance of the war. And that decision would not be long in coming.

Tu Media Group

Adapted from the Alvin Jewett Johnson map of 1862, and showing the new Confederate Territory of Arizona.

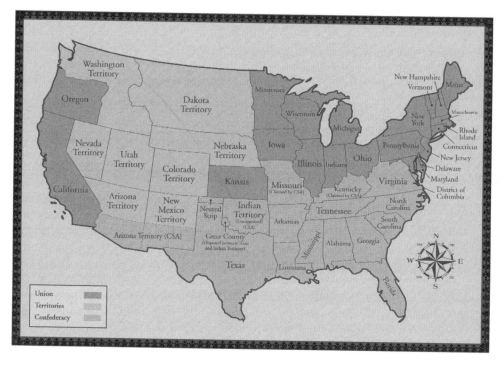

Tu Media Group

Civil War map of the United States of 1863.

# Sibley's New Mexico Campaign and the Second Battle of Mesilla

There were numerous battles around the New Mexico territory in 1862, some of them aimed at either securing or taking Butterfield mail outposts to claim the passage across New Mexico and Arizona to California. But the major battles, those that would decide the outcome in the territories, were between Sibley and Canby, and the first of these, the Battle of Valverde, marked an auspicious beginning for the southern Army of New Mexico.

By early February, Sibley had moved his men north along the Rio Grande to within a few miles of Fort Craig. Not wanting (wisely) to attack the fort directly, he attempted to draw the Union forces out in to battle, but they did not bite at first. Sibley then crossed the river (to the east side) and established a vantage directly across from the fort. Some of Canby's spies attempted an assault on the Rebel forces by wiring up a couple of donkeys with explosives and sneaking them into the camp at night. Unluckily for them, the animals were loyal and followed them back out of the camp, where they exploded—the spies survived; the donkeys did not. The battle itself began on February 20th when Sibley had men press northward and back toward the river to a spot called the Valverde Ford, in an attempt to cut off Fort Craig from Santa Fe. Canby responded by sending out troops to confront the Confederates.

> After crossing all his men, Canby decided that a frontal assault would fail and deployed his force to assault and turn the Confederate left flank. Before he could do so, though, the Rebels attacked. Federals rebuffed a cavalry charge, but the main Confederate force made a frontal attack, capturing six artillery pieces and forcing the Union battle line to break and many of the men to flee.[lxxxvi]

In the end, Sibley won the two-day battle in the sense that he held the battleground, causing Canby's troops to retreat to the confines of the fort. When Canby flew a white flag, Sibley assumed it meant surrender was imminent; Canby though only meant it " . . . for the purpose of ceasing hostilities to enable the dead and wounded to be removed and cared for."[lxxxvii] If Sibley did indeed win the day, the victory was somewhat pyrrhic. Fort Craig was not captured and Sibley lost some 8% of his troops -- 36 dead, 150 wounded, 1 missing.[lxxxviii] Canby suffered greater losses than that, but held the fort.

Sibley was free then, however, to continue north on his way to Santa Fe, the capture of which would give him effective control of all of the New Mexico and Arizona territories. He would only get as far as Albuquerque. Canby, rather than pursue, kept his forces at Fort Craig to disrupt supply lines between Sibley and El Paso. The situation would remain taut and unresolved for another month, until Sibley attempted to move on Santa Fe where he would be met by federal forces from Colorado that had marched down from Denver in remarkable time. Sibley in fact did surprise these forces, commanded by a Union Colonel named John Slough, at Glorieta Pass, to the southwest of Santa Fe, and seemed to have the upper hand at first. The skirmish played out in a narrow pass called Apache Canyon, with the Confederates trying to hold high ground, but ultimately being forced to retreat. Though casualties were not terribly high, many men were lost as prisoners. The main battle took place on March 28. Slough, against Canby's orders, engaged the main Confederate force in a long battle that ended without a clear winner, though with Sibley's forces holding the battlefield.

What changed everything was the somewhat lucky encounter by flanking Union forces of the main Confederate supply train, which was decimated. Without supplies, the southern forces had to begin a retreat back to Albuquerque and then south along the Rio Grande. The retreat marked the turning point in the battle for New Mexico. A large contingent of Union volunteers from the west, called the California Column, were soon to arrive in New Mexico, making it impossible for the South to make another attempt at the territory.

On the way back to El Paso, these Confederate troops were involved in one more skirmish—at Mesilla. Although it wasn't much of a battle, it marked the last confrontation between the Confederate and Union forces in New Mexico. The fact was that, on this retreat, the Southern forces found their reception in southern New Mexico much different they had on the way north. The citizens, especially the Mexicans, were now hostile to these forces, forcing them to forage and steal for provisions. On July 1, a raiding party entered Mesilla and tried to steal cattle. They were separated, and some of the raiders were then confronted by locals. "In a desperate attempt to cross the river and return safely to their camp at Las Cruces, all but one of the Confederates were killed, including their commander . . . "[lxxxix]

So ended the Southern occupation of New Mexico.

Tu Media Group

Post Civil-War map of the Arizona and New Mexico territories (showing Doña Ana and Mesilla Counties covering southern NM.

# Martial Law, the Rise of the River and the Beginning of the Fall of Mesilla

New and unpleasant forces were to arise in the wake of the Confederate occupation, none welcomed by the citizens of Mesilla. And indeed, this period during the rest of the war and after was to mark the high point of Mesilla as a burgeoning city. One need only look at the population to see that this is so—by the time the war began, there were around 3000 residents in and around Mesilla. A hundred and fifty or so years later, those numbers have not really changed. Las Cruces on the other hand has grown from a small town to a city of 100,000.

Upon the arrival of the California Column, the New Mexico territory was secured for the duration of the war. There were fears, not unfounded, that Sibley, who had retreated to Fort Bliss and then San Antonio, was attempting to put together a large enough contingent of men to re-take New Mexico, but given the size of the force now occupying the territory, that attempt never came close to happening. But it was enough of a fear that, once the California Column, under command of Colonel (soon to be Brigadier General) James Henry Carleton, took control of southern New Mexico down through El Paso, Carleton, who had become the commander of the Department of New Mexico, declared martial law. He also set about taking care, once and for all, of the Indian problem. In both cases, he ruled with an iron fist. The effect of Carleton's rule in Mesilla itself would be hard felt—there were plenty of people left behind there, as throughout the territory, who had either been vocal supporters of the Confederacy or were perceived as having been so. And these folks were to suffer under the new occupation.

For one thing, Carleton ordered Colonel Joseph West, the commander of the post at Mesilla, " . . . to strip the Mesilla Valley of all excess food provisions in order to discourage Baylor's plan to retake the territory."[xc] Carleton then ordered, " . . . all suspected Southern sympathizers in the vicinity [to] be detained, marched north to Fort Craig, and their property destroyed."[xci] Sympathizers were also stripped of real estate, a fact that decimated a number of previously successful Mesilla citizens. One was Rafael Armijo, who owned a building in the middle of the stage block south of the plaza. He was convicted of treason and his real estate, along with nearly $40,000 in goods and cash, were confiscated.[xcii] So too with Roy Bean, who would years later become the famous Texas judge. He had bought, from his brother Sam, the property on Calle de Parian directly across from the southern end of the plaza. He too was convicted of treason and saw that property confiscated[xciii] It's even possible that Bean had left Mesilla before that happened, retreating with the Confederates as they went back to Texas.

Mesilla was a different place after the war than it had been before.

In these same years, as the war played itself out and the occupation dragged on, the river decided to rear its angry head again and change things once more for the residents of Mesilla. The river had always, in between drought years, been subject to cycles of flooding and receding in the spring. "Time after time the bocacequias were destroyed and heedless waters ripped up new fields. Countless times the men of La Mesilla and the other river colonies were called to ditch duty or fatigas."[xciv] But from 1862 to 1865, a series of particularly heavy floods beset the area. Silt from the riverbed was carried around and deposited in various places, causing new lakes to form, covering fields and ruining crops. Toward the end of this cycle, in 1865, the flooding was so violent and the silt deposited so deeply that it partly closed off the old river bed that had run between Mesilla and Las Cruces since the early 1840s and dug itself an entirely new bed well to the west of Mesilla, beneath the rise to the mesa. But the bed to the east still, apparently, at least some of the time, held enough water that Mesilla itself became an island. It's not clear exactly how often or to what extent Mesilla was surrounded, for there were still years when the river dried up entirely, or nearly so. But on February 1, 1866, the year after the large flood, the Mesilla Ferry Company was chartered.[xcv] It would have certainly been used to maintain traffic between Mesilla and Las Cruces, and so clearly the water to the east persisted and remained an on-going problem. Residents seemed also to have attempted to deal with it in other ways, though the timeline of these efforts isn't clear either:

> [Post-1865 ] [t]he valley is described as one vast sheet of water from the edge of Las Cruces to the hills on the west, with the site of La Mesilla a strip of island. It is said that for years the river actually ran into this bend, keeping the water high and almost deadly to inhabitants. However a movement of the people, headed by the *Mayor-Domo*, dammed up the mouth, and in a few years the stagnant water had evaporated, and people began to take up their residence in the valley and farm lands upon the rich deposit area of the former river bed.[xcvi]

In some of the years after this, drought struck again, finding new ways to kill the crops and ruin farmers. In other years there was more flooding, isolating Mesilla again. This cycle, from an island to a sand-blasted wasteland, continued until 1885 when another huge flood was to mark the area. After this flood, the river settled permanently in its western bed. It wasn't long after this that serious talk began to arise about the possibility of a dam upriver though that would not become a reality for many years.

The key aspect to the timing of this flooding and the periodic isolation of Mesilla, surrounded as it was by sandy lowland, would come to bear late in the next decade, of the 1870s, when the Atchison, Topeka and Santa Fe railroad was deciding exactly where to run its tracks down through the valley.

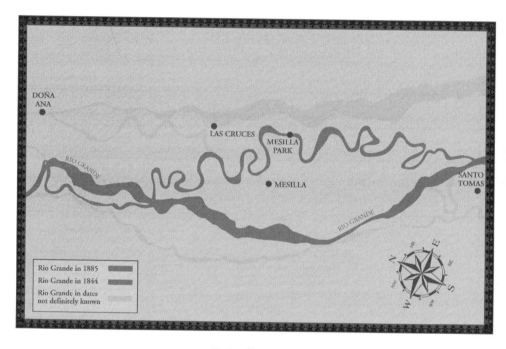

Tu Media Group

Map giving some idea of the various channels the Rio Grande held during the years of the middle 19th century.

Branigan Memorial Library Photographs; Courtesy of New Mexico State University Archives and Special Collections

"Old Mesilla After the Flood."

# From the Riot on the Plaza to the War on the Range

The 1870s in Mesilla dawned with the town having actually avoided most of the terrible violence of the Civil War. The flooding and drought and the occupation were not pleasant things but the battles themselves had really been little more than skirmishes. This new decade, however, was to be a violent one in its own right, beginning with a political skirmish that grew badly out of hand and ending with the range wars to the east that would see one of the most famous trials of the era brought right to the Plaza in the heart of town.

The summer of 1871 witnessed an intense political campaign in the region for the election of the New Mexico territorial representative to the federal Congress. Mesilla was still at that time the Doña Ana county seat as well as one of the region's largest towns and its center of political activity, so the campaign would surely make stops there, as it did in other venues in the area.

One of the large issues behind the tension in the region was that of land, specifically the old Spanish and Mexican land grants that were poorly documented and being targeted now by local businessmen. Most of these were Republicans, backed by a group of judges, lawyers, businessmen and others out of Santa Fe called The Ring.[xcvii] The current landowners and those who had been or were being forced off of their land organized as well, and some prominent locals, including Thomas Bull (who we have seen before) and John Lemon, were part of that group. Interestingly, Bull would later become a leader of a new group called the Democratic Club, while Lemon would take on a leadership role in the local Republican party and later be nominated for a judgeship. [xcviii] Another source of anxiety was a rumor that Texans were going to come back into the area, as they had after Guadalupe Hidalgo, and try to claim land as well. This fear was exacerbated by the priest Jose Jesus Baca who exhorted " . . . his Mesilla parishioners to vote for Republicans, who he thought would do a better job of protecting their lands than Democrats, who he linked to the

Anglo Texans who had come into the area in large numbers."[xcix]

In the build up to the election these tensions were all seething beneath the surface. Loud arguments broke out at rallies in towns around the area including in Las Cruces. In the town of Picacho that July violence struck when "a Democrat clubbed a Republican over the head with a pistol."[c] But that situation was calmed down before anyone else was hurt. Not so when it came to a big political rally in Mesilla on August 27, 1871.

The problem in Mesilla on that day was, first, that both parties had scheduled rallies for the plaza, and second that campaign whiskey was flowing. There were hundreds of participants and, though the Republicans had earlier agreed to let the Democrats have the plaza, they gathered at Lemon's house nearby. Such trouble was in the air that troops from Fort Selden had already been on the scene, but as things seemed to be going smoothly, they returned to the fort. "Newspaper accounts say the [Republican] crowd headed out, lead by Lemon . . . and arrived just as Democrats were making a ceremonial march around the Plaza. The two groups were soon marching in opposite directions, yelling and glaring at each other across the plaza, and came to a head in front of the Barela-Griggs-Reynolds store."[ci]

A shot was fired then, not at anyone though it might as well have been. When Lemon confronted one of the Democrats and threatened him, he received a club over the head. He survived long enough to be helped home where he dictated his will. Then he died. Meanwhile, the Democrat who had clubbed Lemon was himself shot to death, and the melee was on.

When the dust had settled, nine lay dead and many more than that were injured. Troops returned from Fort Selden to restore order but the damage was done.

One irony was that Lemon, a Union sympathizer, had very nearly been hanged by the Confederates. He convinced them to spare him, though others were put to death as he watched. Later, after he died in the riot, the man who took his place on the ballot would eventually marry his widow as well.

A number of Mesilleros would ultimately leave the town for other parts as a result of the violence.[cii]


Near the end of the decade another conflict, the Lincoln County War, broke out well to the east of the Mesilla Valley but it would nevertheless have an impact on the town of Mesilla and provide it with one its sharpest and most enduring legacies.

The roots of the conflict are not too complicated. Two men, Lawrence Murphy and James Dolan, controlled most of the commerce as well as the law enforcement—Sheriff William Brady—in Lincoln County at that time. Two newcomers, an Englishman named John Tunstall and a Canadian named Alexander McSween, with backing from the well known cattle baron John Chisum, began ranching in the county and set up a store in competition to the Murphy-Dolan alliance. Murphy and Dolan did not take kindly to that fact. They had a gang of supporters, a small army if you will. Tunstull and McSween had plenty of men too.

Several of the Tunstull-McSween men, including one named William McCarty, aka William Bonney, aka Billy the Kid, were witness to an ambush by a Murphy-Dolan posse that killed Tunstull. This led to the appointment of their own law force in the county, and from that the formation of a group called the Regulators, which, despite the deputization of its members, was essentially a counter-force to the Murphy-Dolan gang. These deputies then would attempt to arrest the Murphy-Dolan gang members who had killed Tunstull.

Ultimately the territorial governor sided with Murphy and Dolan, declaring the Regulator deputies unauthorized, and hence the arrests they made illegal. These arrests had also involved the supposedly justified killing of several of Tunstull's killers. The tinder was dry.

Courtesy of the Palace of the Governors Photo Archives (NMHM/DCA); negative # 009587.

"Street Scene in Mesilla, NM," 1877 – right around the time of
the Lincoln County War.

122

"Street View in Mesilla, NM," June 1881; Courtesy of the Palace of the Governors Photo Archives (NMHM/DCA); negative # 009582

Another street scene in Mesilla, 1881, the year of the Billy the Kid trial.

# The Trial and the Legend
## of Billy the Kid

Not long after this, in the spring of 1878, Sheriff Brady and several of the other Murphy-Dolan gang members—more "deputies"—were ambushed by Regulators in middle of Lincoln, NM. Brady was killed. One of the Regulators present was Billy the Kid. He claimed later to have not even shot at Brady, but rather at one of the deputies, who was not killed. Many years later, in 1936, Susan (McSween) Barber, the widow (since remarried) of Alexander McSween, and a friend of Kid's at the time of the war, told an interviewer, "I understood at the time that Billy said he tried to get Billy Matthews, who was walking with Brady, and did not even aim at Brady."[ciii] Of course this is only the long distant memory of one person who had liked the Kid, and it relies on the Kid's own statements which were likely self-serving to begin with. But it illustrates a larger point about his whole legend, which is that much of it in fact IS legend. So much has been written about Billy, dissecting, re-creating all the moments of his short violent life, that it's hard now to tease out the subtleties of truth.

One thing that seems certain though, in that it comes up again and again in testimonies from those who knew him, is the fact that the Kid was a generally nice guy, happy, always smiling, and well liked by those who knew him—including even the man who would ultimately kill him. But let Mrs. McSween Barber's own words, fifty-five years after his death, illustrate this point for us as well:

> Billy was a graceful and beautiful dancer, and when in the company of a woman he was at all times extremely polite and respectful . . . He was always a great favorite with women . . . It was just natural for him to be a perfect gentleman . . . Billy was not a bad man; that is, he was not a murderer who killed wantonly. Most of those he did kill deserved what they got. Of course, I cannot very well defend his stealing horses

and cattle; but, when you consider that the Murphy, Dolan, and Riley people forced him into such a lawless life through their efforts to secure his arrest and conviction, it is hard to blame the poor boy for what he did. One thing is certain—Billy was a brave as they make them and knew how to defend himself. He was charged with practically all the killings in Lincoln County in those days, but that was simply because his name had become a synonym for daring and fearlessness.[civ]

This is not to imply that Billy the Kid was innocent or that he didn't commit a number of murders. He did. But almost as surely his exploits were exaggerated, perhaps even by those who fought against him.

It's also certain that later in the summer of 1878 there was a large culminating battle between the Regulators and the Dolan-Murphy gang. The Kid and others who had been indicted in the Brady murder were trapped in the McSween house, which, after several days, was set on fire by the Dolan-Murphy forces. Susan McSween and her children were in the house at the time, but managed to escape without injury. So did some of the gang members including Billy.

The Kid went on the lam. At one point though he met with the new territorial governor, Lew Wallace, and was apparently promised some kind of amnesty. So he turned himself in and was promptly jailed indefinitely—that is until he escaped. Stories of rustling and other deaths followed him, and still do to this day. He was cornered again by a posse the next year and escaped.

Also in that year a new sheriff was elected in Lincoln County. Pat Garrett's reputation would come nearly to rival that of the Kid himself, with their destinies to be tied inextricably together.

Garrett finally was able to arrest the Kid in late 1880. Lincoln County authorities filed for a change of venue for the trial because, according to the district attorney who cited, among other reasons, the fact that "...jurors and witnesses in said cause are so intimidated by lawless men in said Lincoln County that the said jurors and witnesses cannot fearlessly perform their respective duties at said trial in said Lincoln County."[cv] Another more salient part of his reasoning may well have been the fact that the Kid was well liked in Lincoln County, and an impartial jury might have been hard to find. Certainly, the Kid's own attorneys fought this change in venue but lost. The trial was moved to what was still, for a short time longer, the seat of Doña Ana County—Mesilla. Bonney was transported there by train and then by wagon. He was tried in the building at the southeastern corner of the plaza, a building that still stands today, known now as the Billy the Kid gift shop. In that humble structure the Kid was convicted of a crime he claimed never to have committed—what turned out to be the only conviction of any participant for any crime committed during the Lincoln County Wars.

Also of great local interest is the fact that, after his arrest, Billy contacted a local Mesilla attorney named Albert Jennings Fountain, a figure who, like Pat Garrett, would go on later in his life to star in an old west drama not unlike those Billy the Kid had been involved in (as we shall see). Fountain was first appointed by the court, then agreed to continue with the case if Billy could pay. While in jail in Mesilla, the Kid wrote a letter to Fountain about Billy's mare, which had been confiscated when he was arrested by Sheriff Garrett. He explained that he would need to reclaim her so she could be sold. Then he could pay Fountain which, apparently, he did.

Despite Fountain's efforts, though, the trial was swift and Billy was found guilty. The judge ordered him taken back to Lincoln County and held in prison until May 13 when, according to the judge's orders, he, in " . . . some suitable and convenient place of execution within said county of Lincoln . . . be hanged by the neck until his body be dead."[cvi] Things didn't happen in quite that way, however.

One last thing we know is that Billy, while he may have been blamed for some murders he didn't commit, he certainly did commit others—at least nine for sure, possibly as many as 21, if some accusations are to be believed. Two of the most egregious, the final two that we know of, were after his conviction in the courthouse on the corner of the plaza in Mesilla and his return to Lincoln. He somehow managed to kill both his guards, to hack off his irons, and to escape yet again.

Though Billy was once more on the lam and in a place where he was known and now wanted, he never went too far. A few months later, in the middle of that summer of 1881, Pat Garrett followed rumors of Billy's presence in or around the town of Fort Sumner, which lies little more than a hundred miles to the northeast of Lincoln. Garrett had watched places Billy might turn up and ended up at Pete Maxwell's ranch. He went into the darkened room where Maxwell, a friend of Billy's, slept, to talk to him. It turns out Billy was using that room as well. As Garret spoke to Maxwell, Billy stepped in, surprising them. One story has it that he had a knife in his hand because he had be going to cut meat, another that he had his gun drawn. Or perhaps it was that when he saw someone sitting there in the dark, he reached for his gun. It is known that he said, "*Quien es?*" Who is it? He may have been asking about Garrett's dark presence in the room, or he may have been asking Maxwell about Garrett's men who were outside. In any case, Garret shot first and then again, killing the Kid instantly.

Garrett would go on to write a book called *The Authentic Life of Billy, the Kid*, which, added to the fact of the killing itself, led to Garrett's own brush with fame—and money. Aside from the book, Garret received other money for his famous deed. A paper at the time said, "Las Vegas gave Pat Garret over $1300, and Sante Fe gave about $600. Every town in the territory should do something to swell the purse. Judge Newcomb telegraphed $50.00 from Silver City. It is expected that $250.00 can be gathered in Las Cruces and Mesilla."[cvii]

Photo reprinted by permission of Frank H. Parrish.

Newly discovered and authenticated photograph of Billy the Kid (on the right) with his friend, Dan Dedrick. Taken around 1879.

"Plaza, Mesilla, NM," 1880-1882; Courtesy of the Palace of the Governors Photo Archives (NMHM/DCA); negative # 014580.

Mesilla Plaza, 1880-1882, around the time of the Billy the Kid trial.

Courtesy of the Palace of the Governors Photo Archives (NMHM/DCA); negative # 009593

"Group at Back Part of Courthouse Showing Where County Jail Was," Mesilla, NM, 1890-1900, taken not too many years after Billy the Kid was held and tried there, around 1890-1900.

"Old Courthouse Building," Mesilla, NM, 1915?; Courtesy of the Palace of the Governors Photo Archives (NMHM/DCA); negative # 105370

Front of the old Mesilla Courthouse, probably around 1915.

[lxix] Taylor, *A Place*, 84

[lxx] Kiser, *Turmoil*, 143

[lxxi] ibid, 144

[lxxii] Perkins, Robert, azrebel.com, "The Forgotten Legacy." Last modified July 23, 2007. Accessed December 21, 2013. http://azrebel.tripod.com/page10.html.

[lxxiii] Kiser, *Turmoil*, 146

[lxxiv] Kiser, *Turmoil*, 153

[lxxv] Charles Walker, "Causes of the Confederate Invasion of New Mexico," *New Mexico Historical Review*, 8, no. 2 (1933). Accessed December 24, 2013. http://westofthemississippi.angelfire.com/articles/causes_of_the_confederate_invasion_of_new_mexico.html

[lxxvii] Kiser, *Turmoil*, 157

[lxxvii] eric@littleblackstar.com, "Confederate Invasion of New Mexico . . . Wednesday, July 24, 1861," *Civil War Daily Gazette* (2011). Accessed December 26, 2013). http://civilwardailygazette.com/2011/07/24/confederate-invasion-of-new-mexico-western-virginia-heats-up/

[lxxviii] Jerry Thompson, "Colonel John Robert Baylor: Texas Indian Fighter and Confederate Soldier," (Hillsboro, TX: Hill Junior College Press, 1971), cited in Kiser, "Turmoil," 265

[lxxix] Lynde as cited in McFie, *History*, 52

[lxxx] Kiser, *Turmoil*, 168

http://www.desertusa.com/mag01/jan/stories/ghost.html

[lxxxi] Martin Hardwick Hall, "Sibley's New Mexico Campaign," (Albuquerque, NM: University of New Mexico Press, 1960), 19

[lxxxii] Jay Sharp, "Ghosts of Old Mesilla," *DesertUSA*. Retrieved 12/28/2013

[lxxxiii] Taylor, *A Place*, 86

[lxxxiv] IKiser, *Turmoil*, 179

[lxxxv] Hall, *Sibley's*, 3

[lxxxvi] American Battlefield Protection Program, National Park Service, U.S. Department of the Interior, "Valverde -- CWSAC Battle Summaries." Retrieved 1/3/14. http://www.nps.gov/hps/abpp/battles/nm001.htm

[lxxxvii] Hall, *Sibley's*, 70

[lxxxviii] ibid, 71

[lxxxix] Kiser, *Turmoil*, 188

[xc] Kiser, *Turmoil*, 194-195

[xci] Kiser, *Turmoil*, 196

[xcii] Thomas, *La Posta*, 40

[xciii] Thomas, *La Posta*, 38

[xciv] Taylor, *A Place*, 110

[xcv] George B. Anderson, "History of New Mexico: Its Resources and People, Volume II," (Los Angeles, CA: Pacific States Publishing Co., 1907), 1031

[xcvi] McFie, *History*, 49

[xcvii] Eric Fuller et al, "Shootout in La Mesilla," *Southern New Mexico Historical Review*, Doña Ana Historical Review, Volume XX, January 2013, 8. Retrieved online January 17, 2014. http://www.donaanacountyhistsoc.org/

HistoricalReview/2013/SNMHR2013shootoutinMesilla.pdf

[xcviii] Fuller, *Shootout*, 9

[xcix] Denise Holladay Damico, "El Agua es la Vida: Water Conflict and Conquest in Nineteenth Century New Mexico," PhD dissertation, Brandeis University, 2008. Retrieved 1/18/2014, http://books.google.com/books?id=VgjF-Pv8CZ0C&printsec=frontcover#v=onepage&q&f=false

[c] Fuller, *Shootout*, 10

[ci] Christopher Schurtz, "Deadly Politics: Mesilla Plaza Site of Worst Political Riot in NM," *Las Cruces Sun News*, 10/2/2010, accessed 1/18/2014, http://www.lcsun-news.com/las_cruces-news/ci_16238587

[cii] Schurtz, *Deadly*

[ciii] Miguel Antonio Otero, Jr, "Chapter 8 - Echoes of the Lincoln County War," in *Billy the Kid: The Best Writings on the Infamous Outlaw*, edited by Harold Dellinger, 121-132. Guilford, CT: Twodot Book Publishing, LLC, 2009, 127

[civ] Otero, *Echoes*, 125-126

[cv] Theron Trumbo, from various sources, "The Courts and Early Lawbreakers" (chapter), from "A History of Las Cruces and the Mesilla Valley," Historical Data Committee of the Centennial . . . 1949 (Theron Trumbo, Chairman), typescript held in Special Collections, New Mexico State University Branson Library, 98

[cvi] Trumbo, *Courts*, 99

[cvii] Trumbo, *Courts*, 100

# Part V

## Struggles and a New Birth

# The Railroad and the Rise of Las Cruces

That spring of 1881 was really a perfect moment in the history of the town of Mesilla, marked by a confluence of the most famous people and events of that time in that place and the arrival of the force that would seal it's end as the most important place in the southern territory. It was a sort of coming together before it came apart -- Albert Fountain, William Bonney, Pat Garrett, all were there. And even as the Kid was leaving town, the railroad was arriving.

By early 1881, the Atchison Topeka & the Santa Fe Railroad (AT&SF) had built a line south as far as Rincon, which then angled to the west, toward Deming. At the same time, the Southern Pacific was building a line east from California toward Deming as well. When they met in March of that year the second fully transcontinental railroad line in the United States had been created. The Southern Pacific would then continue on eastward toward Texas. It had contemplated coming all the way east from Deming to Mesilla before turning south to El Paso, but in late 1880 Leland Stanford himself, the head of the railroad, decided finally that that was a waste of track—the distance to El Paso could be made fourteen miles shorter by cutting the corner south of Mesilla. [cviii] Meanwhile, however, the AT&SF had built a split at Rincon, and while one spur led west to Deming, another kept on due south, directly through the heart of the Mesilla Valley.

Note how Billy the Kid was transported from Lincoln (via Santa Fe) to his trial in Mesilla—he was brought by train to a spot north of Las Cruces, probably near Fort Selden, that was the end of the line, and then by wagon the rest of the way. The tracks had not quite reached Las Cruces, though they were close. The Kid arrived at the Mesilla jail on March 28, 1881.[cix] On March 23, tracklayers were working at Fort Selden; they were expected in Doña Ana by the first week of April,[cx] the same week the Kid's trial would commence. The track would reach Las Cruces on April 26, 1881 -- after the Kid's conviction and return to Lincoln for hanging, and just about the time of his escape. By the time of his capture in July, the balance of things in Doña Ana County had already shifted.

As recently as the end of 1880, plans had still been that the AT&SF line would go through or very near the town of Mesilla—a business periodical of the time called *The Public* stated in its December 23, 1880, issue that, "At latest advices it [the AT&SF] had laid track 25 miles south from San Marcial, New Mexico, having only about 75 miles more to be laid between that point and a junction with the Southern Pacific near Mesilla, on the Rio Grande."[cxi]

If one reads the standard histories, it seems that the reason the railroad came through Cruces instead of Mesilla is a settled matter. Most texts or articles give the stock response that people in Mesilla, for some reason, were not friendly to the railroad, and that people in Las Cruces welcomed it with open arms. Or perhaps that the landowners of Mesilla were holding out for more money. A piece in a manuscript put together by the Historical Data Committee of the Centennial . . . 1949, says, " . . . the owners of the land [in Mesilla] refused to sell, declaring that they wanted nothing to do with the railroad. It is rumored that this attitude was taken in an effort to force the Santa Fe to pay more for the land than it was actually worth."[cxii] Rumor being the ultimate source of the information. It's a nice pat answer, perhaps too pat. The reality of the situation was almost surely more complicated, having to do not only with money but also with the nature of the land itself.

It is true that the railroads in general, and certainly the AT&SF, were looking for free or low cost passage wherever they could find it (or take it). It is also true that a group of businessmen in Las Cruces banded together to form the Las Cruces Town Company, which donated land (mostly owned by the Armijo family) to the railroad right of way. Undoubtedly this played into the railroad's hands. But it is also hard to believe that the businessmen of Mesilla would have been hostile to a rail line that they would have known would lead to the town's further prosperity. It may be that they wanted to be paid for the right-of-way, while the Las Crucens were willing to donate land. If so, the Crucens were certainly more prescient than the Mesilleros. But it also makes sense, looking at the situation logically and from an engineering perspective, that the railroad would have had a strong motivation to come through Cruces rather than Mesilla. This is for the simple reason that Las Cruces lay on higher ground and, as has been pointed out, the flooding and isolation of Mesilla had continued from the time of the Civil War. Why, if you're running tracks, would you fight with the unpredictable river and sandy bogs and arroyos, when you could come through on higher drier ground?

And there's no question that flooding was a big problem for the AT&SF.

As late as 1905, there appeared in the professional trade periodical *The Railway World* this notice: "In the expectation of escaping further flood damages, the Atcheson, Topeka and Santa Fe is planning to rebuild its tracks on higher ground in the Mesilla Valley, north of El Paso, and extending toward Albuquerque, NM."[cxiii] It's not clear exactly where these troubled spans were but the river was still a big problem. In another example, a description of the 1884 arrival in the Mesilla Valley of Mary Bloom (mother of Elizabeth McFie Bloom, who has been quoted numerous times in this account), includes this passage:

> The train was going through a flooded area, and twenty-four year old Mary Bloom, the youngest of seven sisters, began to regret her husband's decision. Why had he given up the speakership of the Illinois House of Representatives to come to this godforsaken place where the river had washed away the county seat at Mesilla, so that the land-office papers had to be moved by boat to Las Cruces, getting soaked in the process."[cxiv]

And so, extrapolating back to late 1880 or early 1881, it makes complete sense that railroad engineers, on surveying the territory they were soon to be crossing, would have felt strongly that the land through Cruces was more desirable to their task than that through the regularly flooded bosque around Mesilla. That the Las Cruces Town Company was willing to give land to the cause would have just made the decision that much easier.

In any case, it marked the abrupt end of Mesilla as the political center of the Mesilla Valley. In 1882, Las Cruces was declared the new county seat of Doña Ana. A few years after that, the Las Cruces college, forerunner to New Mexico State University, was founded.

It was during this time that a second church in Mesilla – this one Episcopal – was formed. A house was purchased in 1877 and part of it turned into a chapel. It was called the St. James Mission, later to be known as St. James Church. The ministers were largely missionaries during this time though in 1889 Fr. Henry Forrester oversaw the construction of a larger adobe building.[cxv]

By the early 1880s the larger church was already aware that the town of Mesilla was not perhaps the ideal place for its investment. An 1883 report on its domestic missions stated:

> The town of Mesilla has gone down since the railroad passed through. If it could have been foreseen, the money could have been much better invested in several other places. But at the time the purchase was made . . . Mesilla was one of the most thriving places in New Mexico. It was thought then it would be, what El Paso has since become, the railroad centre for that part of the country.[cxvi]

The church remained in Mesilla until 1900, when it was relocated to Mesilla Park, where it stands today.

# Albert Fountain's History of Mesilla

In 1885 or so, Albert Fountain, his fame and political career rising from his role in the Billy the Kid trial, wrote a short history of Mesilla, about nine hand-written pages. A few curiosities surrounded the document. Why, to begin with, was it written in Spanish? Fountain's Spanish was certainly good (his wife, after all, was Mexican) but not perfect. In addition the writing was flowery in places, a little ornate. Also, the document is housed in Albuquerque, at the Center for Southwest Research at the University of New Mexico, rather than with the rest of his papers in the archive at New Mexico State University in Las Cruces.

It turns out that, in all likelihood, Fountain wrote the document for a very specific purpose that lead both to its style and its fate. At that time, the territorial government of New Mexico maintained an Office of Immigration – apparently to encourage people, including Mexicans, to move into the sparsely populated state. People of note in the various towns and other locales around the state were approached by the department to write what amounted to ads promoting life in their corner of New Mexico. Many of these were published and distributed by the department. One can only surmise that Fountain was approached as the representative of Mesilla. His piece, however, was never published, and so ended up in a government file somewhere in Albuquerque or Santa Fe, and eventually in the archive.

A new collaborative translation is provided here. It should be noted that the original document was badly stained, especially on the later pages, so that some of the text was unreadable. The translators were able, using context and other clues, to largely re-create Fountain's meaning, though some small liberties have been taken to provide a complete document and a few small gaps still exist.

# Compendium of the History of the Picturesque Town of La Mesilla[cxvii]

## By Albert J. Fountain, Jr.

La Mesilla, situated in the Southern part of the Territory of New Mexico, in the County of Dona Ana, is a picturesque town of interesting historical events of a happy past, and it is destined to a bright future. Her fertile lands that are enclosed within La Merced de la Colonia Civil de La Mesilla [the Mesilla Colony Grant], were, have been, and will always be the magnet of everyone who loves a happy home. And to our famous valley was given the name El Valle de La Mesilla. To give a fair idea of this historic village, I present some details.

In the year 1851, there were 300 families from El Paso del Norte (now Ciudad Juarez), as was happening in other parts of Mexico and Nuevo Mexico, who came to colonize La Merced de La Mesilla, accompanied by the commissioner of the Mexican government, Rev. Father Don Ramon Ortiz. Amongst the many colonizers figured Don Ramon Gonzales, Rafael Bermudez, Rafael Ruila (Ruelas), Anastasio Cisneros, Eugenio Moreno, Marcial Padilla, Cristobal Ascarate, Isidoro Armijo, etc.

Once established, the town and the lands were marked out two fields to each colonist. The acequia of San Albino was constructed, and the land was planted in great part with wheat, corn, beans, tobacco, etc. Within two years, the fertility of the land sparked a general enthusiasm and in fewer than two years the population doubled. La Mesilla had gained great prestige.

Through the Treaty of Guadalupe Hidalgo of February 2, 1848, the Territory of New Mexico and all of Alta California was ceded to the United States of America.

The Rio Grande, which in those years ran to the east of La Mesilla Plaza, divided la Merced of Dona Ana to the east, and La Mesilla to the west of the Rio Grande, serving as the same an international boundary of both governments.

The gold fields of California were discovered the same year of 1848, and the entire world traveled in pursuit of the gold of fortunate California. As a result, in 1849 Las Cruces was populated and this in brief led to Las Cruces becoming the capital of the Dona Ana County, by an act of legislation on the 31st day of December of 1852.

Through the Gadsden Treaty, the United States of America in the year 1854 acquired all that part to the west of the Rio Grande all the way to the Alta California, and in September of 1854 at the Plaza of Mesilla, Engineer Salazar and General Angel Frias [sic], with his guard of honor and his troops which accompanied him, General Mor[r]is, his guard of honor, and the troops from Fort Fillmore represented the United States.

A crowd of people from Dona Ana and Las Cruces assembled, with great enthusiasm, in the Plaza of La Mesilla, to witness the Ceremony of the Intrega [transference] from the Mexican government to the government of the United States of America of the land encompassed by the purchase of the Gadsden Treaty.

Above a leafy Cottonwood located at one corner of the Plaza of La Mesilla the glorious emblem of the stripes and stars was hoisted and the representative of Mexico, in an eloquent speech, transferred the sold land to the United States of America, and explained to the town that the mother country had sold that land, but to her inhabitants, according to the Treaty, was given the privilege that within one year of that date they could declare if they wanted to continue as Mexican citizens or to adopt the new country with equal rights of American citizens. This was verified with a few and very rare exceptions.

That was the day of glory, and the music, the great dance, and the sumptuous banquet followed, and the town of La Mesilla rose proudly, shining the new diadem of her acquired natural resources. This made her the most suitable route to California. That same year the Overland changed its principal depot to Mesilla. Merchants from different parts came to establish great houses of commerce, vineyards, hotels, and offices of various types.

On December 31st of 1855 the legislature declared La Mesilla the capital of Dona Ana County. This act won her the title of chief city of Dona Ana County and the population of this emerging town grew in a marvelous manner.

In 1861, the Civil War in the United States was declared. The government requested volunteers and La Mesilla, even though she had only been an adopted daughter for six years, had the honor of offering more that her quota of soldiers. The Confederate Troops had taken possession of the town in 1861, but the Federales [Union troops] later expelled them in a struggle that was fought in the town. Later, as the Confederates withdrew, General West came a few days later with his column of volunteers from California. Amongst them were Col. W.L. Reynorson [sic], David Wood, Col. A.J. Fountain, and Mayor Barncastle, who, afterward, settled in Mesilla. It was a time of happiness for our town. The farmers sold their product at very good prices and everyone made money.

The first cloud that came to darken, to some extent, the glories of La Mesilla was the war or political skirmish that took place in the autumn of the year 1871 where retinues of Republicans and Democrats found themselves in the heat of political battle and then confronted each other in a shootout which lasted the entire day until a company of soldiers from Fort Selden came to restore order. There were more than thirty wounded from one side or another, and about nine deaths including the Honorable Don Juan Limon. Due to this occurrence a great number of families left the town of La Mesilla, some to colonize the towns of Asuncion, Mexico, [   ], Colorado, Tularosa, New Mexico, etc.

Shortly after the ruin that was caused by these political altercations, the Santa Fe Company had arranged to establish its depot in La Mesilla, but the owners of the land refused, at any cost, to sell the land, declaring that they did not want anything to do with the railroad company. This incited a progressive spirit of my never-forgotten Honorable Jacinto Armijo who offered half of his land so the depot could be set in Las Cruces, which was accepted. And in the year 1883 the capital of the county was moved to Las Cruces until today.

An act that the town of Las Cruces should never forget is that that noble man was in reality the father of the progress of Las Cruces and if gratitude would allow them, they should raise a monument in his memory. The effect of his donating the land for the depot in Las Cruces was in reality the death of my beloved town after thirty years.

But as truth and justice can never be killed, the natural resources of La Mesilla have made new life, and today we, who always have known her true merits, can see with happiness the new dawn of a growing future in her fertile and not to be equaled valley.

Today, thanks to the generous help of (our priest) Rev. Padre Juan Granger, who contributed more than $8500.00, we have a church that cost close to $15,000.00. We have a public school that cost $11,000.00 [...] and will have a population of close to 700 children!

There is so much more that can be written about this picturesque town and I hope to have the time to write it, so that the local readers and the tourists can understand that this, a now sleepy town, has been a town with interesting events, and is destined for a brilliant future.

A.J. Fountain, Jr.

# The Long and Twisted
# Path Continues

The violent outbursts of the 1870s and 80s may seem at first blush small blips on the great expanse and history of the Mesilla Valley and the broader territory of New Mexico. But they were more than that.

First, they were indicators of the tone of that time. This was a place that, quite suddenly in the late 1840s, with the signing of the Treaty of Guadalupe Hidalgo, became open to all Americans. And the Americans who tended to come to such a wide-open place were adventurous and ambitious to say the least. But they were moving to a land in which a culture had been percolating for many hundreds of years, a culture that was slow and easy and trusting, and left itself wide open to the aggressions of the newcomers. And so these outbursts were not one-off of random occurrences, but in fact were harbingers for what was still to come. By the mid-1890s the New Mexico territory and the Mesilla Valley itself were not past the terrible violence that had marked them so far.

Second, these acts of violence—riots and range wars and murders and hangings and shootings—were what broad swaths of the rest of the country saw as indicative of this place. The Wild West was a real thing, and the heart of it beat in Mesilla, NM. One of the upshots was that, when it came to considering New Mexico for statehood, this was the reputation that preceded the place. Not the whole reputation, but certainly a part of it, and that had a deleterious effect on the efforts legislators were making.

In fact, that road had begun as long before as 1850, not long after Guadalupe Hidalgo.

At that time, remember, one complication was that Texas claimed its territory ran all the way to the Rio Grande. If that was so, and Texas was already a state, then what would a state of New Mexico look like? Another problem was that a New Mexico constitutional convention passed a resolution promoting statehood but also banning slavery. This was a sticky issue at the time, as we have seen in events leading up to the Civil War. The upshot was that Congress passed the Compromise of 1850, which, among other things, withdrew Texas's claim to New Mexico land to the Rio Grande, but in a deal with the southern delegation, declared New Mexico and Arizona to be territories, thus preventing New Mexico from becoming a non-slave state.

Time and again after this, various reasons would crop up behind the territory's failure to achieve its aim of statehood—reasons that changed as the times changed around it. When the southern part of the territory became, for a time, one of the key pieces of the Confederacy, the mood in Washington toward statehood grew muted. Still later, opposition came from groups within New Mexico whose self-interest was served best by maintaining territorial status. The reason for this was that, as a territory, administrators were assigned by Washington and were often Republicans. It was feared that if the state became self-determining, the native population would sympathize more with Democrats.

By the late 1880s the view of the region as unfit for statehood had come to focus on the people themselves. This was partly due to the violence associated with the region, as pointed out. It was also frankly due to in no small part to a broad xenophobia, the view that the "Mexico" part of New Mexico was a problem, that this was land with a non-American culture, non-American people, and of little value agriculturally. It had mineral value, but its status as a territory didn't stop that from being exploited.

One need only look at some representative newspaper and magazine comments of the time to see how New Mexico was regarded by the rest of the country. In a 1943 essay in the New Mexico Historical Review, Marion Dugan collected a number of quotations and citations regarding the views of the rest of the country in the late 19th century toward New Mexico. A few follow:

From the *Las Vegas Optic,* July 9, 1891:

The Territory of New Mexico is to the masses of America a terra incognita. If they have ever heard of it the knowledge is of a place luxuriant with cactus, sagebrush and vast areas of sand: a land in which water is at a premium, and life holding on by its eyebrows. The capitalist recognizes in such a country no opportunity for investments; the farmer never thinks of it as inviting his labor by offering remuneration and competency, and the laboring man generally passes over the land as unworthy of consideration.[cxviii]

From the *Albuquerque Morning Democrat* in June, 1895:

The misconceptions in the east are more numerous about Arizona and New Mexico than any (other) part of the west today. Even very intelligent people believe the whole country an uninhabitable desert, and it will take lots of advertizing [sic] to persuade them the country is really what it is.[cxix]

From Clarkson N. Potter, a New York Congressman,

This is a territory of slow growth, not of rapid growth. Its population is composed mainly of descendants from Mexicans. The business of legislation in the territorial Legislature is carried on, I am informed, largely by means of an interpreter, as is also business in its courts. A very considerable portion of the population of the Territory do not speak the English language. It seems to me that these are all reasons why, so far as the interest of New Mexico is concerned, she has now less claim than another Territory with no more population might [have].[cxx]

And from the *Albuquerque Journal-Democrat*, March 17, 1901, citing James McGuire, mayor of Syracuse, New York:

He had observed that eastern capitalists and home seekers were afraid of territories. The general impression prevailed that the people were wild and lawless and incapable of governing themselves. Though a territorial form of government might be as good, or even better in some cases, the fact that people thought it wasn't would prevent and investments.[cxxi]

Sadly, the violence that had marked territory up to the point of the mid-1890s was to continue to mar the reputation of the territory of New Mexico into the new century.

# The Strange and Tragic Disappearance of Albert Fountain

By the 1890s, Albert Fountain was firmly established as a pillar of the Mesilla community. Well before his defense of William Bonney made him famous in the region, and in fact more widely than that via telegraphed reports from the "Wild West," he had already been a Texas state senator and lived a life of adventure and danger that could form the basis of half a dozen wild westerns. He served in the California Column during the Civil War (which is how he ended up in New Mexico), was sentenced to execution by a firing squad, found himself cornered by Indians in a canyon and shot by arrows, got shot in a bar fight (and was saved by a sheath of papers and his pocket watch), and fought Indians with the Mesilla Scouts, which he had organized. In the time after the Billy the Kid trial, Fountain had continued to build his legal career, and a political one as well. He became an assistant U.S. District Attorney, under which guise he fought, among other groups, the Sante Fe Ring mentioned in the Riot chapter.

In 1888, he ran against a man named Albert Fall for a seat in the New Mexico legislature, and won. A few years later, Fall received a judgeship in the 3rd district. This political battle was a harbinger of the dynamics that would play out over the rest of Fountain's life, both in terms of his accomplishments and his enemies:

> Fountain pushed for public education for both boys and girls, an unpopular idea at the time. He successfully fought to have the state's land grant college situated in Las Cruces. . . . He also fought vigorously for statehood. The rest of Fountain's life would be intertwined with that of his opponent in the 1888 election. The two men, Fountain as a leader of the Republicans and Fall as a soon-to-be leader of the Democrats, grew to despise each other.[cxii]

Oliver Lee was a cattle rancher with land located south of Alamogordo, on the eastern edge of the Tularosa Basin (a small part of his enormous ranch is now the Oliver Lee State Park). He was also, it is widely accepted, a cattle rustler, known for stealing the range cattle of other large operations and rebranding them to appear as his own. Judge Fall appointed Lee, a friend and client, and two other associates of theirs, James Robert Gilliland and William McNew, as Deputy U.S. Marshalls. When Fall was forced to resign from the bench for improprieties, these appointments were no longer valid, but the sheriff Fall had previously helped get elected stayed in office, and he named Lee, Gilliland and McNew his own deputies. So, although they were criminals, they had the patina of the law around them—much like what had happened in the Lincoln County wars of the 70s.

Fountain was hired by a large cattle group, the Southeastern New Mexico Stock Growers' Association (of which, ironically, Lee was a member), to prosecute these crimes.[cxxiii]

And so the sides were set—Fountain and the stock association on the one, and Fall, Lee, Gililland and McNew on the other. Fountain gathered plenty of evidence and was seen as a direct and immediate threat by the rustlers. In January of 1896, Fountain left Las Cruces with his youngest son, Henry, accompanying him, and headed east by wagon 150 miles to Lincoln where there was to be a hearing into the matter of the cattle rustling, and where Fountain would attempt (and succeed) to obtain indictments against Lee, Gilliland and McNew. There was some concern for Fountain's life by his family and others because of threats he had received. It's possible that he took Henry as a kind of protection—who, his wife, Mariana, had wondered, would try to kill a man who had a child with him?[cxxiv]

In an interesting coincidence, the courthouse in Lincoln where Fountain secured the indictments was the same one Billy the Kid had escaped from fifteen or so years earlier, before being killed by Garrett. Though he had received another death threat during the hearing, Fountain finished his business and then, carrying the indictments, Fountain and his son headed back west toward the White Sands and then Mesilla, stopping during the three-day trip to stay with friends in the cold weather. Fountain noticed, and was later told by a postal carrier he knew, that men were shadowing him—first two, and then three horsemen. The postal carrier encouraged Fountain to come with him to friends for the night, but Fountain refused, wanting to get home – he had promised his wife he'd be home for dinner, and Henry had a bad cold. Alongside present-day Route 70, perhaps 30 miles east of Las Cruces, not too far north of the broad curve north that 70 goes through after it passes the entrance to the White Sands Missile Range, a New Mexico historic plaque marks the approximate spot where Fountain and Henry vanished. What is surmised, as well as supported by the evidence of blood and horse tracks that led back to Lee's ranch, is that Fountain was shot in an ambush by the men he was seeking to prosecute. It may also be the case, again based on blood evidence, that little Henry's throat was cut after the wagon and horses were led or run off of the main road. The bodies have never been discovered.

Another coincidence or irony is that one of the men called in to investigate the horrible crime was none other than Pat Garrett. He along with other investigators including Pinkerton agents gathered evidence that seemed to indict Lee and the others. This led to a kind of repatriation of Garrett to New Mexico—he was appointed sheriff of Doña Ana county by the governor in the year of the disappearance and spent much of his time investigating it. After three years, there was another trial, this in Hillsboro, to the north of Mesilla. But due to lack of evidence and probably legal charades, in a trial in which Albert Fall himself defended Lee, Gilliland and McNew, none of the three was found guilty. All were released.

Courtesy of Jay W. Sharp / desertusa.com

Courtroom of Lincoln County Courthouse, where Fountain secured indictments of Oliver Lee and his men, and where he received a hand-written note threatening his life if he proceeded.

Image No: 02220021; Courtesy of New Mexico State University Archives and Special Collections

Group of judges and prosecutors in front of the Doña Ana County courthouse, May 30, 1891. Colonel Albert Fountain, assistant United States attorney, is in the front row, second from the left.

# Judge Barnes

In an interesting aside to the story of Albert Fountain, Dr. Edwin Burt, the great-great-grandfather of the author of this book, C.W. "Buddy" Ritter, became one of the first non-military surgeons in Mesilla. In an ironic wink of fate, his office turns out to have been the two rooms in the front of the Double Eagle Restaurant that now serve as Mr. Ritter's own offices. Mr. Ritter did not know this at the time he purchased the Double Eagle in 1983.

Dr. Burt 's son-in-law — Mr. Ritter's great-grandfather — was Richmond Palmer Barnes, later New Mexico Supreme Court Judge Barnes. Judge Barnes was hired by Albert Fountain's widow to help prosecute the case at Hillsboro. He was quite an orator and during closing arguments was noted to have "quot[ed] freely from Dickens' *Pickwick Papers*."[cxxv] Some of the jurors, non-English speaking Mexicans, had trouble following the translations of Barnes' expressions. But this gift for language certainly was an asset in his long and illustrious career as a lawyer and a judge.

Some years later, Judge Barnes wrote a letter to his daughters (the elder of whom, Margaret, would be Mr. Ritter's grandmother). The letter provides such an intimate and unexpected insight into the life of that time in and around the Mesilla Valley, and provides such astute advice, that is has been reproduced here in its entirety.

Deming, N.M.T., Oct 25, 1908

Dear Margaret and Bess:

I came down here night before last to try a case against Mrs. Carpenter and her Mex. Employee, Monico, for killing a calf belong to the Wilson boys. We worked hard all day yesterday, and examined only one witness, partly finishing with another. At this rate, we will be half of this week getting finished.

It is a very nasty case, but we expect to clear Mrs. C., at least, and think we can clear the Mex. There is undoubtedly a conspiracy behind the prosecution, but it will be hard to prove. Today is Sunday and I slept late this morning, as I have had to try to get rest in cold beds for a week past. The weather has been unusually cold all through N.M., and I have been sleeping in cold rooms at Mogollon and the Gila; so, last night as the weather had moderated, I had just a bully sleep and feel rested today. Mr. Harllee is here, too, but will go home today, and may not come back for this case. Mr. Hamilton, a lawyer of Deming is also in the case so I shall have help anyway.

I have a great many letters from you all, and know what you are doing and how you are situated, and it is all very jolly and delightful, I think. The house and neighborhood where you are now must be all you could expect and I am glad you are there. Mama seems to find the Washington relatives something of a disappointment. I presume that they are. Relatives are seldom much good, anyhow, they belong to the wrong families, I guess. Mrs. Veazey is delightful, I am sure. Please give her and Mrs. Borden my warmest regards. I should like to hear something from you as to your schools, and what you are doing in them. Is the Arts and Crafts any good, and what are you working on Bess? Talk with one of your sensible teachers and get a list of technical and descriptive books about their work and read them if you can get he time. What you should work for, I think, is some line or specialty that you feel a real interest in, and then make a sincere study of it. And if you are to take up interiors, you must study it from an historical standpoint, for it is a very largely a question of periods and styles founded and classified by those periods. For the sake of your own mental and artistic development it will pay you to be more than merely superficial, and instead of cutting you off from social enjoyment, it will add an otherwise unobtainable zest to it. Know something, and know it well, and you will then be sought after and looked up to. It will mean work and some self-denial for a time, but you will thank every star that ever shines on you in after life, if you do this, and will be surprised how your path will broaden as you meet allied subject along the known road. If you don't know one thing thoroughly you can never have a starting point from which to attack other things.

It is the same in music for Margaret. Get down to its history and schools. Learn what its masterpieces are and why. All at once you will find you know something, and you will respect yourself and other people will be bound to grant you respect. Mind, and its development are all there are in life that last – we have to start early, but we learn how greatly they are worth the labor later. Also, I wish you would go on with Spanish. Get what books you need, and some of the books should be good, light novels; and I think a good rule would be to use that language altogether when you are at home with the others of the family. Mama has outstripped me in study, excepting in my profession and in general reading, and, in the last line my reading has been quite too general, I am afraid.

Now, enough of this. It isn't a lecture, I think of you all and what you are doing every hour of the day, and I want you to do something and do it right. It won't be much to you now, but it will be much to you in after years. And all the material you need is right at your hand in Wash. Your grandfather can help you to it, if you will talk with him, and he can get you entrance to the Govt. libraries, if you find difficulty alone.

There really isn't much news to write you. I have skimmed all the cream of it into the short notes to mama. The Smiths left the house about a week ago, a little more, and I have not seen them since. I think the trouble was that Macy had a room there with me, and that he disturbed Mrs. S., who is very nervous, by coming in at all hours of the night and then rummaging about for books. I did not think he was so real of a nuisance, but I reckon he is – still, his head is worth all the trouble his vagrant body makes. I am not sorry, tho, as Mrs. S. turned out to be a very sick woman. I shall have her personal room, which she stayed in nearly all the time, cleaned and fumigated, and try to get another tenant. Rod. is well, and comes up almost every night to see me. The cat came back to Mrs. Coon's, but had an ulcer on it neck, and she has had him, as well as the cat of the same family killed. Cost me a dollar, but it had to be done.

Business is quite good and something new comes in every week. Money has been hard to get, tho, and that is why you have had to wait a bit for your winter clothes. The Comanche case is not settled yet, but expect it will be with be next two weeks. Will know more about it and have something more definite to write as soon as I get home. Mr. Lowe, of the bank, has been to Milwaukee, and has had the bank claim of $38,000 settled and paid. We will get a comm. on that as well on about $30,000 of other claims. The delay has been occasioned by a fight brought on by the Milwaukee people over the amount of the Receiver's and Referee's fees. Which they wish to cut in two.
I am writing this in Mr. Fielder's office. He is prosecuting the case agst. Mrs. Carpenter most viciously, but we will hold him down. He is pretty well; and sends his love to all of you, not forgetting mama. It is a beautiful, warm day here, with no wind or dust. I hope you are having an equal day, there. I hear we have a new Episcopal clergyman in Silver, but I have not met him, yet, as I have been away from home the last

three Sundays.

Love to mama, and each of you give her and Virginia a big kiss for me. I miss you all more than you could believe, but I know it will be work while, your stay there, and I am not complaining even a little bit. I know you are busy, but write when you have time.

Your loving daddy,

Judge Barnes lived until 1946. This is his obituary from the State Bar Association of New Mexico:

Richmond P Barnes, former State Supreme Court Justice and one of New Mexico's oldest practicing attorneys, died in Albuquerque, November 11, 1946. He was 87 years of age, but despite failing health for several years, had continued his law practice until about a month before his death.

Judge Barnes was a native of Carthage, NY and came to New Mexico in 1885, settling in Mesilla and later moved to Silver City where he practiced law in the office of Conway and Posey. He moved to Albuquerque in 1915 after serving as a member of the 33rd Territorial Legislature from Grant County in 1897 and as District Attorney of the Third Judicial District from 1899 to 1900. He was a member of the state legislature from Bernalillo County in 1917 and 1919 and was appointed to the State Supreme Court in 1928.

He is survived by three daughters, , Mrs. Winfield F. Ritter of El Paso, Texas, Mrs. Frank Coon of Albuquerque, and Mrs. M P Walker of Tucson AZ and a son C B Barnes of NY City.

Judge Richmond P. Barnes

Dr. Edwin Burt

Guadalupe Street, 1900, with San Albino in the distance. The horse and buggy would have been parked about in front of today's Double Eagle restaurant.

# The Life and Death of a Lawman

The end of the violent period of life in the New Mexico Territory and the Mesilla Valley seemed to come, in historical terms, with one final definitive and symbolic act that occurred only a few months before the writing of Judge Barnes' letter. Again, the ironies abound, as you will see.

Pat Garrett had helped build his own legend after he killed the Kid with the publication of his book *The Authentic Life of Billy, the Kid.* Oddly, Garrett's law enforcement career did not flourish in the years after that. He lost several elections for sheriff and eventually relocated for a time to Texas, not really returning to New Mexico for any appreciable stretch until the disappearance of Albert Fountain. The subsequent investigation saw Garrett re-instated, as it were, when he was appointed Doña Ana County sheriff.

Garrett's pursuit of Lee and the others, especially Gilliland, in the lead up to the Fountain trial is the stuff of yet more western legend. The two men had encountered each other in a saloon before the arrest warrants came down and were painfully courteous to one another. But this barely hid what was beneath the surface.[cxxvi] Lee's claim was that Garrett intended to do exactly to him as he had done to Billy the Kid—that is, not to arrest him at all but to assassinate him. Garrett denied this wholeheartedly and said he was only trying to make arrests in the case, but he also knew Lee would not come willingly and saw him as a killer. In fact, "Lee and Gilliland [took to] hiding out in the desert, with beards grown fully for disguise."[cxxvii] Albert Fall, meanwhile, left the region for some time. The pursuit came to a head a year before the trial, in July of 1898, at a place called Wildy Well on part of Lee's property but some distance from the main house. Lee and Gilliland had been spotted at the ranch of W.W. Cox, Lee's brother-in-law, by a couple of Garrett's deputies.[cxxviii] Garrett and his posse cornered Lee and Gilliland at Wildy Well, but Lee got the upper hand, having taken refuge on the roof of the house and, in a shootout, badly injuring one of Garrett's men. Lee would later claim that it was Garrett who had set up an ambush, taking shots at him with no warning. Garret of course denied that, and claimed that he had called out to Lee and Gilliland several times to surrender.

It was blow to Garrett that he had to retreat with his men without taking the injured one, who would die a day or so later.[cxxix] In time, as the trial approached, Lee and Gilliland would surrender. But how they did that, and to whom, makes another interesting side story in the violent history of the region. There was already some political pressure to create a new county in southern New Mexico, with Alamogordo as its seat. Now that proposition would also prove to be expedient to Lee and Gilliland, if it were to pass—and since Albert Fall was one of those negotiating for the new county, it happened. This was accomplished by removing the political opposition of the governor, Miguel Otero, when the offer was made to name the new county after him. He changed his position "almost overnight."[cxxx] Otero now had a county—created from parts of Dona Ana, Lincoln and Socorro counties—and, lo and behold, the new county line fell to the west of the spot where Albert Fountain and his son had disappeared. This meant that the jurisdiction was no longer Dona Ana County, but the new Otero County. And the sheriff of this new county, George Curry, was an old friend of Fall's. It was to him that Lee arranged to surrender, avoiding Garret and the Dona Ana County jail altogether. (It's interesting to note that Curry himself would later become governor of New Mexico.)

In 1899, Garrett was involved in another killing that may have marked for him the end of his time as a lawman. It happened, coincidentally, on the same ranch where Garrett's deputies had earlier spotted Lee and Gilliland—that of William "W.W." Cox, Lee's brother-in-law, though the case in question didn't have anything to do with Lee or that history. Garrett and a deputy had tracked a murderer from Oklahoma to this ranch and cornered him. When he fought (bashing Garrett in the head) and got to a gun, they killed him. The death was attributed to the deputy, and neither he nor Garrett was held to blame. Though Cox wasn't happy about what had happened on his property, there was apparently no bad blood then between him and Garrett, who later worked with him on a roundup.[cxxxi]

By the next year, Garrett's law enforcement career was at an end. The money was terrible, for one thing, and Garrett had to actually bring a suit against Doña Ana County to get what was owed to him. In addition,

> . . . Pat was rapidly tiring of the sheriff's life. Now nearing fifty, he was too old to be spending so much time in the saddle. He wanted different work, something free from financial difficulties. With the dismissing of the territorial case against Lee, Gilliland and McNew, his prospects vanished for a share of that reward money. The work of five years had been for nothing."[cxxxii]

Garrett did not seek re-election.

In 1901, after having led a delegation to El Paso to meet with President McKinley to discuss, among other things, statehood for New Mexico, Garrett was then appointed by Theodore Roosevelt (after McKinley's assassination) as Collector of Customs in El Paso. This job paid substantially more than the sheriff's position in Doña Ana County, and Garrett served in it for five years. He later apparently embarrassed Roosevelt by having him pose for a photo with a known gambler in San Antonio, and afterwards was not re-appointed.

Garrett still had a ranch in New Mexico, not far east of the San Augustin Pass, just to the north of the Organ Mountains. It was to this place that he retired but, according to most accounts, the financial difficulties that had temporarily been alleviated by the post in El Paso now returned. In the end, by 1908, Garrett was in danger of losing the ranch and leased it to none other than William Cox, who promptly arranged to have a man named Jesse Wayne Brazel used it to graze goats. When Garrett learned of the goats, he protested, knowing they would ruin the land for cattle. He then arranged to sell the ranch to another man, Carl Adamson. Adamson and Garrett were in a wagon on the way into Las Cruces on February 29 when Brazel accosted them. What happened next is subject to some conjecture even now, but whether Brazel (who was charged with the crime) fired or whether there was another assassin lying in wait, Garrett ended up dead besides the wagon, a bullet having passed through his head. Though Brazel claimed Garrett was going for a gun, evidence seems to suggest that he was in fact urinating. Brazel was defended by the infamous Albert Fall and was acquitted of the crime.

A plaque along Route 70 just east of Las Cruces commemorates Garrett's death though the spot he was actually killed upon is marked by a different cruder marker of his son's making. Garrett is buried in the Masonic Cemetery on Compress Road in Las Cruces.

PAT F. GARRETT
The most famous peace officer of the Southwest

public domain

Garrett near the end of his life, around 1907.

U.S. Senate Collection, Center for Legislative Archives

"Senatorial Filibustering," by Clifford K. Berryman,
Washington Evening Star, January 31, 1903.
"During the late 19th Century various members of Congress introduced bills
in support of Arizona and New Mexico statehood, but none were approved.
In 1903 the Senate Committee on Territories reported a bill to enable Okla-
homa, Arizona and New Mexico to be admitted into the Union. Senator
Matthew S. Quay (R-PA) pushed to pass this Omnibus Statehood Bill but was
blocked by Senator Albert J. Beveridge (R-IN) in the "Senatorial turnstile."[cxxxiii]

# The Evolution of the Church

The San Albino Church, at the north end of the Plaza in Mesilla, is widely known to have existed as two buildings, the first giving way to the second in 1906 - 1908.  But in fact the building seems to have gone through four distinct phases. The original church was housed in a simple jacal from its founding in the early 1850s until the first formal building went up in 1857.  No photos of the jacal exist, of course, but there is a photo below of a typical jacal that San Albino might have looked like.

The building erected in 1857 existed in that form until the middle 1880s when it was extensively remodeled, including the addition of a single enclosed bell tower or spire.  That building existed until 1906, when the current building, with two spires, was erected in its place, and opened in 1908.

Image No. 00040373; Amador Family Papers; Courtesy of New Mexico State University Archives and Special Collections

Jacal home constructed of wood, branches and mud, near Las Cruces, ca 1900

"The Catholic Church of San Albino (built 1852), Mesilla, New Mexico," Original 1881, Stiles and Burke; Courtesy of the Palace of the Governors Photo Archives (NMHM/DCA); negative # 014299.

San Albino before the restorations of the mid-1880s. This was taken in 1881, so this is the original building erected in 1857, with an open bell tower that wasn't there after the restoration. The bell may not have been present in this building until 1876.

"The First San Albino Catholic Church (built in 1852) Under Restoration, Mesilla, New Mexico,"
Date Original 1885 – 1890; Courtesy of the Palace of the Governors Photo Archives (NMHM/DCA);
negative #122144

San Albino undergoing restoration, 1885-1890. The single enclosed bell tower
is being erected here.

San Albino Catholic Church, ca 1896; Image No. 00040319; Amador Family Papers; Courtesy of New Mexico State University Archives and Special Collections

San Albino around 1896, with its single enclosed bell tower.

San Albino Catholic Church, 6-Nov.; Image No. 00041314; Amador Family Papers; Courtesy of New Mexico State University Archives and Special Collections

Another view of the reconstructed church, after mid-1880s and before 1906.

The newest version of San Albino Basilica opens in 1908. This is the building
that still stands today.

"Plaza at Mesilla, NM," Date Original 1890-1900?; Courtesy of the Palace of the Governors Photo Archives (NMHM/DCA); negative #014578

A crowd on the Plaza, in front of the former Maurin – Leonart Building with the new San Albino Basilica in the background – so the actual date of this photo has to be sometime after 1908.

# A State at Last

Though Garrett's death had no direct bearing on New Mexico's seemingly endless quest for statehood, it does seem to mark a particular moment in time—the end of the bloody period of the settling of the Mesilla Valley and the rise and fading of Mesilla itself. And whether by coincidence or in part because of this fact, it was not much longer that the territory had to wait for its acceptance, finally, into the United States.

Still, the quest had dragged on through one strange iteration after another.

In 1902, Congress took up a bill to bring Oklahoma, New Mexico and Arizona into the union, and rather than speculating about odd and foreign territories, members of a Senate committee actually toured New Mexico to see and hear from her citizens. . . The bill died in the Senate the next year, but two years later statehood popped up again – this time with a proposal to bring New Mexico and Arizona into the union as one state, known as "Montezuma". . . .The rationale for "Montezuma" was that combining Arizona's smaller population with New Mexico's larger population would constitute a more appropriate congressional representation than if they were admitted separately. New Mexico's territorial delegate, Bernard Rodey, made the case that the two territories contained distinct populations and were separated by a mountain range. That proposal died, but it came up again the next year.[cxxxiv]

One of the rationales for the name Montezuma was to get rid of the name Mexico. It was believed, probably correctly, that having Mexico in the state name put off a number of easterners, who saw it more as a part of that country than this one. In 1905, statehood was nearly achieved when a "jointure" bill again linked New Mexico & Arizona as a single state—this time to be called Arizona. It received legislative & presidential support, but the Arizona territory rejected it, fearing New Mexican political and economic dominance because of New Mexico's larger population.

As the quest for statehood wound on, life went on in Mesilla itself. In 1906 construction began on the new San Albino church, which actually incorporated parts of the old building within it. It was dedicated in 1908, still before the arrival of statehood.

On June 20, 1910, President Taft signed an Enabling Act allowing the New Mexico territory to call a constitutional convention in preparation of its anticipated statehood. A hundred delegates met in Santa Fe in September, 71 Republicans including all of the 33 Hispanic delegates and 29 Democrats. A constitution was written, and approved by voters in the new year. And yet still there were delays. In August of 1911, because of a provision in Arizona's constitution allowing the recall of judges, President Taft vetoed a combined statehood bill for Arizona and New Mexico.

At last, in January of 1912, Taft proclaimed New Mexico the 47th State to enter the Union. The President signed the proclamation at 1:35 p.m. and smilingly said: "Well, it is all over. I am glad to give you life. I hope you will be healthy."

Almost 64 years after the signing of the Treaty of Guadalupe Hidalgo, the territory was brought into the Union. William McDonald, a Texan, was named our first Governor. The legislature elected Albert Fall and Tom Catron as U S Senators.

Arizona, which frequently disagreed with NM in Congress, became the 48th state on February 14,1912. But of all the contiguous territories of the Union, New Mexico had remained a territory the longest and attempted Statehood the most – 47 times during a 66-year struggle.

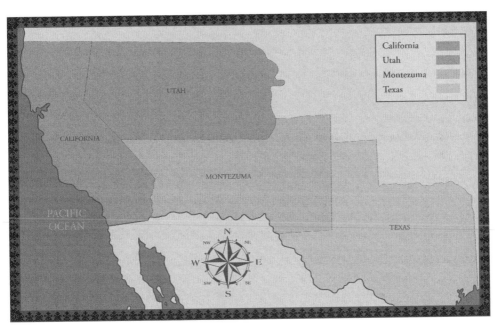

Tu Media Group

What the proposed state of Montezuma would have looked like.

U.S. Senate Collection, Center for Legislative Archives

### "Admission to Statehood," by Clifford K. Berryman, *Washington Post,* May 24, 1911

On June 20, 1910, Congress passed an act to authorize the people of the New Mexico and Arizona Territories to form constitutions and state governments, and provide for the admission of the states into the Union once those constitutions were approved by Congress. After the Territories held constitutional conventions and had their constitutions ratified by the people, each Territory submitted their new constitution to Congress. Arizona's constitution, however, contained a provision for the recall of judges—a provision which was opposed by many members of Congress as well as by President William H. Taft.[cxxxv]

**TERRITORY OF NEW MEXICO.**

**OFFICE OF THE SECRETARY.**

**CERTIFICATE.**

I, George H. Wallace Secretary of the Territory of New Mexico, hereby certify there was filed for record in this office, at 4-55 o'clock P. M. on the twentieth day of March A.D. 1901, Join t Memorial No. 5, petitioning Congress f r dmission of New Mexico as a state,

and also, that I have compared the following copy of the same, with the original thereof now on file, and declare it to be a correct transcript therefrom and of the whole thereof.

In Witness Whereof, I have hereunto set my hand and affixed my official seal this twenty-eighth day of March A.D. 1901.

*Geo. H. Wallace*
Secretary of New Mexico

Resolution from the Territory of New Mexico petitioning Congress for the admission of
New Mexico as a state, March 28, 1901

*Records of the U.S. House of Representatives*
*National Archives*

BY THE PRESIDENT OF THE UNITED STATES OF AMERICA.

A  PROCLAMATION.

------------

WHEREAS the Congress of the United States did
by an Act approved on the twentieth day of June,
one thousand nine hundred and ten, authorize the
people of the Territory of New Mexico to form a
constitution and State government, and provide for
the admission of such State into the Union on an
equal footing with the original States upon certain
conditions in said Act specified:

AND WHEREAS said people did adopt a constitution and ask admission into the Union:

AND WHEREAS the Congress of the United States
did pass a joint resolution, which was approved on
the twenty-first day of August, one thousand nine
hundred and eleven, for the admission of the State
of New Mexico into the Union, which resolution required that the electors of New Mexico should vote
upon an amendment of their State Constitution, which
was proposed and set forth at length in said resolution of Congress, as a condition precedent to the

President William Howard Taft's Proclamation for the admission of New Mexico as a
State into the Union (page 1 of 3), January 6, 1912

General Records of the U.S. Government
National Archives

admission of said State, and that they should so
vote at the same time that the first general election as provided for in the said Constitution
should be held:

AND WHEREAS it appears from information laid
before me that said first general State election
was held on the seventh day of November, one
thousand nine hundred and eleven, and that the
returns of said election upon said amendment were
made and canvassed as in section five of said
resolution of Congress provided:

AND WHEREAS the Governor of New Mexico has
certified to me the result of said election upon
said amendment and of the said general election:

AND WHEREAS the conditions imposed by the
said Act of Congress approved on the twentieth
day of June, one thousand nine hundred and ten,
and by the said joint resolution of Congress have
been fully complied with:

NOW THEREFORE, I, WILLIAM HOWARD TAFT, President of the United States of America, do, in ac-
cordance with the provisions of the Act of Congress and the joint resolution of Congress herein
named, declare and proclaim the fact that the
fundamental conditions imposed by Congress on the
State of New Mexico to entitle that State to admission have been ratified and accepted, and that

President William Howard Taft's Proclamation for the admission of New Mexico as a
State into the Union (page 2 of 3), January 6, 1912

*General Records of the U.S. Government*
*National Archives*

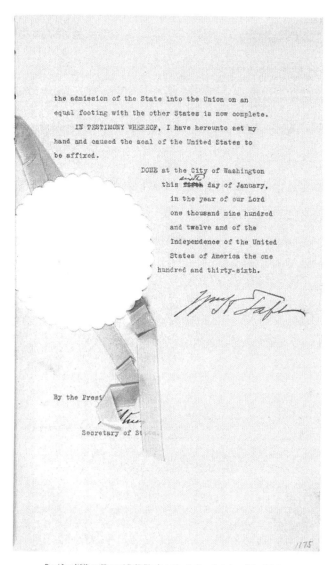

the admission of the State into the Union on an
equal footing with the other States is now complete.

IN TESTIMONY WHEREOF, I have hereunto set my
hand and caused the seal of the United States to
be affixed.

DONE at the City of Washington
this sixth day of January,
in the year of our Lord
one thousand nine hundred
and twelve and of the
Independence of the United
States of America the one
hundred and thirty-sixth.

By the Presi

Secretary of St

*1175*

President William Howard Taft's Proclamation for the admission of New Mexico as a
State into the Union (page 3 of 3), January 6, 1912

*General Records of the U.S. Government*
*National Archives*

184

cviii David Devine, David. "Slavery, Scandal, and Steel Rails," (Lincoln, NE: iUniverse, Inc., 2004), 201

cix Patrick H. Beckett, "Las Cruces, New Mexico 1881," (Las Cruces, NM: COAS Publishing and Research, 2003), 105

cx Beckett, *Cruces*, 114-116

cxi "The Week - Dec. 23, 1880," *The Public*, vol. XVIII, July 1 - Dec. 31, 1880. New York, NY: The Financier Association, 406. University of Chicago Library. Accessed January 30. 2014http://books.google.com/books?id=LV09AQAAMAAJ&pg=PA406&lpg=PA406&dq=why+atchison+topeka+avoided+mesilla&source=bl&ots=Dlx3Sy3b42&sig=l7t96LiZzA6s_ONTUVUYpyR3m88&hl=en&sa=X&ei=6hHYUvKzJKLcyQHW-oG4CQ&ved=0CFAQ6AEwCA#v=onepage&q=why%20atchison%20topeka%20avoided%20mesilla&f=false

cxii Theron Trumbo, from various sources, "Section 18" (untitled), from "A History of Las Cruces and the Mesilla Valley," Historical Data Committee of the Centennial . . . 1949, 85
Railway World, volume 49, No. 1, Jan. 6, 1905, New York, 499

cxiii Ted Morgan, "Shovel Of Stars: The Making of the American West 1800 to the Present" (New York: Touchstone, 1995), 447

cxv From "The History of Our Mesilla Valley Church," St. James Episcopal Church, Accessed April 2, 2014, http://www.saintjameslc.com/history.html.

cxvi "The Spirit of the Missions," The Domestic and Foreign Missionary Society of the Protestant Episcopal Church in the U.S. of America, Volume 48, 1883.556 http://books.google.com/books?id=07TSAAAAMAAJ&printsec=frontcover&dq=spirit+of+the+missions,+episcopal+vol.+48&hl=en&sa=X&ei=uYl1U6_DMIeKqgbbhILwAg&ved=0CDQQ6AEwAA#v=onepage&q=mesilla&f=false

cxviii Original full-draft translations by Rocio Vela and Denise Chavez. Consulting translation / interpretation / compilation by Cheryl Nim, Denise Chavez, Margaret Ritter and Craig Holden.

cxviii Cited in Marion Dagan. "Advertising 'The Backyard of the United States'," New Mexico Historical Review, 18, no. 1, January 1943, pgs. 60-96. See footnote #2. Accessed February 1, 2014. Reprinted on http://www.newmexicohistory.org/centennial/Statehood/Statehood-6.html

cxix Cited in Dagan, *Advertising*. See footnote #4

cxx Congressional Record as cited in Dagain, *Advertising*. See footnotes #17 – 21

cxxi Cited in Dagan, *Advertising*. See footnote #9

cxxii Corey Recko. "Murder on the White Sands: The Disappearance of Albert and Henry Fountain" (Denton, TX: University of North Texas Press, 2007), 11

cxxiii Recko, *Murder*, 12

cxxiv Recko, *Murder*, 20

cxxv Leon C. Metz, "Pat Garrett: The Story of a Western Lawman" (Norman, OK: University of Oklahoma Press, 1974), 224-225

cxxvi William A. Keleher, "Fabulous Frontier, 1846-1912" (Santa Fe, NM:

Sunstone Press, 2008 -- originally published in 1962 by University of New Mexico Press), 252

cxxvii Recko, *Murder*, 108

cxxviii Keleher, *Fabulous*, 253

cxxix Metz, *Garrett*, 210

cxxx Metz, *Garrett*, 214

cxxxi Metz, *Garrett*, 237-239

cxxxii Metz, *Garrett*, 239

cxxxiii U.S. Senate Collection, Center for Legislative Archives http://www.archives.gov/legislative/features/nm-az-statehood/berryman-1903.html

cxxxiii Leslie Linthicum, "New Mexico's Path to Statehood Often Faltered," *New Mexico Travel*, October 23, 2013. Accessed February 2, 2014. http://www.abqjournal.com/286241/travel/new-mexicos-path-to-statehood-often-faltered.html

cxxxv U.S. Senate Collection, Center for Legislative Archives - National Archives and Records Administration http://www.archives.gov/global-pages/larger-image.html?i=/legislative/features/nm-az-statehood/images/berryman-1911-l.jpg&c=/legislative/features/nm-az-statehood/images/berryman-1911.caption.html

# Part VI

## The Mesilla Plaza – A National Historic Landmark

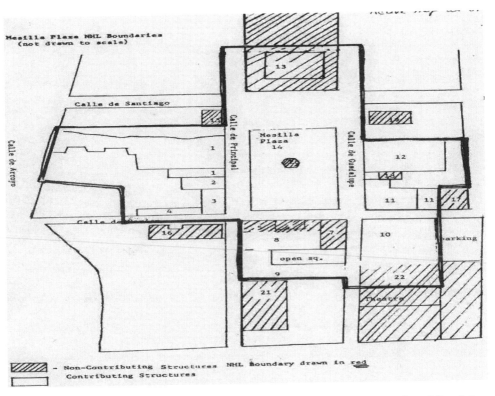

NPS Form 10-900-a
(3-82)

OMB No. 1024-0018
Expires 10-31-87

**United States Department of the Interior**
National Park Service

# National Register of Historic Places
# Inventory—Nomination Form

Continuation sheet         Item number   10       Page   3

Appendix A

Contributing Structures

| | Name | Date | Use |
|---|---|---|---|
| 1. | Taylor Residence | ca. 1850s | Shop/residence |
| 2. | Mesilla Book Store | ca. 1857 | Shop/residence |
| 3. | Leonart–Maurin Store | ca. 1863 | Shop |
| 4. | Leonart–Maurin Residence | ca. 1850s | Shop |
| 8. | El Patio/Restaurant | ca. 1855 | Bar/Restaurant |
| 9. | Stage Depot | ca. 1850s | Restaurant |
| 10. | La Posta | ca. 1850s | Restaurant/Shop |
| 11. | Old Courthouse/Jail | ca. 1850s | Shop |
| 12. | Double Eagle | ca. 1849 | Shop |
| 14. | Plaza | ca. 1849 | Plaza |

Non-Contributing Structures

| | Name | Date | Use |
|---|---|---|---|
| 5. | Transportation Block Shop (5, 6, and 7) | ca. 1850s; modified 1920s | Bar/Liquor/Vacant |
| 13. | Church | 1906 | Church of San Albino |
| 15. | Residence | ca. 1950s | Residence |
| 16. | Residence | early 1860s; Modified 1980s | Residence |
| 17. | Gift Shop/Gallery | ca. 1900 | Shop/Art gallery |
| 18. | Residence | ca. 1940s | Shop/Residence |
| 19. | Residence | 1920s | Residence |
| 20. | Bandstand | 1976 | Bandstand |
| 21. | Storage | ca. 1920 | Storage |
| 22. | Residence | ca. 1940 | Residence |

## The Taylor Residence – Building 1

The Taylor Residence was constructed in the 1850's from adobe brick and adobe plaster, two commercial properties are separated by a zaguan, or interior corridor, which leads to a enclosed patio. Behind extends a long linear arrangement of rooms, that stretch to a barn and stable for the entire block. In the 1850's, a mercantile store, north of the zaguan, was operated by Mariano Yrissari and, after the Civil War, by Marino Barela, both prominent native New Mexican traders. The façade with brick coping and the pedimented lintels capping the windows and doors are examples of the Greek Revival architecture which was adapted in New Mexico to create the "Territorial Style".

## The Reynolds Griggs Building – Building 1A

Constructed in the 1850's from adobe brick and adobe plaster, the Reynolds Griggs Building was part of the commercial enterprise until acquired by the Reynolds and Griggs Company in the 1870's. The façade of the building was changed adding the cast iron front, the metal bracketed cornice, the cast iron roof with the flag pole over the cornice. Extremely high plate glass windows, which cover most of the buildings façade, frame a recessed entrance composed of doors made of glass panes and wood panels. The store, formerly for dry goods, was joined to the company's feed and grocery division by a large arched opening. The new facade reflected a different style from the adjoining Taylor residence indicating the growing influence of the Americans on Mesilla.

## Mesilla Book Center – Building 2

Constructed of adobe brick and adobe plaster, the Mesilla Book Center dates from at least 1857. The façade was added in the 1870's and reflects the Greek revival architecture which was adapted into the New Mexican "Territorial Style." The front part of the building was the south half of the Reynolds and Griggs Company building as served as the feed and grocery division. Edward Griggs, partner in the mercantile, had a residence directly behind this building.

OIHSF

## Maurin and Leonart Store – Building 3

Starting in 1859, Augustin Maurin used burnt brick from his own kiln located about a half mile away for the store. Maurin and partner Eugene Leonart, both from France, designed for a second story as evidenced by the partially completed windows above the level of the canales. With its high parapet and burnt brick coping, the building retains its original look. Leonart left the Mesilla Valley when the Confederate troops withdrew in 1862.

## The Leonart-Maurin Residence – Building 4

Built in the late 1850's as their residence by Augustin Maurin and Eugene Leonart, partners in the adjoining store, the one-story stuccoed adobe brick building has a flat roof parapet, wood framed windows and rough timbered lintels. The viga ends visible indicate the low level of the original ceiling. Maurin acquired much property and influence after the Union troops entered the Mesilla Valley in 1862 but was mysteriously murdered in this building in 1868.

**El Patio – Building 8**

Built in 1855, the one-story adobe building is described in an 1868 deed as a "large adobe house built in the form of a hollow square containing a store-room, a bar and a billiard room" owned by Joshua. Located in the "Transportation Block" the building served as an additional rest stop and waiting room for the several stage lines, which were located in the adjoining building. During the Confederate occupation, The Mesilla Times was published here and later, during the 1860's and 1870's The Mesilla News was published here.

## The Stage Depot – Building 9

The center of the "Transportation Block," this building constructed of adobe in the mid 1850's, was home to the short-lived San Antonio Mail stage line (1857), also known as the "Jackass Line" for their choice of animal to pull the stage-coaches. From 1857 to 1861, it was the Butterfield Overland Stage Depot waiting room and stage offices. They were succeeded by the Wells Fargo stage line.

## La Posta Restaurant -- Building 10

Continually occupied by residences, stores, a blacksmith shop, a winery and a tannery since its construction in the 1850's. It became the Corn Exchange Hotel in the 1870's. The adobe two building complex is of a classic territorial style with a zaguan leading into an enclosed patio. It has brick coping on the parapet, and wood frame windows with pedimented wood lintels. The exterior structure maintains its historical integrity. In 1939, "Katy" Camunez started La Posta restaurant and quickly established a reputation as a wild and wonderful hostess.

## Doña Ana Co. Courthouse and Jail – Building 11

Built originally as a jacal in the early 1850's, that was replaced by a stuccoed adobe building in the early 1860s. The roof is flat with a parapet capped by a dentiled brick coping. The building served as town hall, jail, school and courthouse, until 1885 when the county seat was transferred to Las Cruces.   Col. Albert Fountain served as defense attorney for many notorious trials here. His theatrical speaking style made trials public entertainment events. William Bonney, alias Billy the Kid, was tried here in 1881 and convicted of murder. He was moved to Lincoln where he escaped and was later gunned down by Lincoln County Sheriff Pat Garrett.

## The Double Eagle – Building 12

The Double Eagle is the oldest building on the Plaza, built in 1849. Valentin Maese raised his family in a two room jacal. The house expanded in the 1860's, 70's and 80's to a large rambling Territorial Style adobe structure with walls 24 inches thick. Some of the earliest and most prominent families, the Maeses, Guerras, Valencias and Gamboas, resided here. The façade and inner courtyard have portales constructed with corbels and zapatas (corbelled brackets). The wood frame doors and windows have decorated wood pediments. It has a flat roof with a parapet and capped dentiled brick coping. The rear portion was squared off, with no damage to the original structure.

## The Basilica of San Albino – Building 13

At the north end of the plaza stands the Basilica rebuilt in 1906 -'08 on the site of an 1850's adobe church. It is built of fired brick in the Italianate Style, with belfry façade on each corner. Leaded stained glass windows depicting saints line the walls of the nave. The parapet between the belfries bears resemblance to Mission Style. Both the interior and exterior walls were stripped of their plaster during a 1960's renovation and stabilization. The bells continue to send their signals.

**The Mesilla Plaza**

In 1957, the Mesilla Plaza was declared a New Mexico State Monument because of its historical significance in both the history of the State and the history of the United States. The Plaza was listed on the National Register as a National Historic landmark in January 1982. Mesilla's Historic district was added to National Registry in February 1985. When the Taylor home, gifted to the State of New Mexico, is transferred the State Monument, rangers will staff the Plaza and the Home.

## About the Authors:

**C.W. Buddy Ritter** is a fifth generation native of Mesilla and Las Cruces. He studied at Tulane, received his graduate degree from NMSU, and did post-graduate work at Michigan State University, becoming the first Certified Hotel Administrator in the state of New Mexico. Over the course of 53 years he has owned four hotels, eleven restaurants and two breweries in New Mexico and Arizona. He is currently the owner of Peppers and the Double Eagle on the Plaza in Mesilla. His office in the front of the Double Eagle was once the surgical suite of his great-great grandfather Dr. Edwin Burt, who arrived in Mesilla in the 1870s and is pictured in this book.

**Craig Holden** is the author of six novels, including *Four Corners of Night* (Delacorte), which won the Great Lakes Book Award and, most recently, *Matala* (Simon & Schuster). He received his graduate degree from the University of Montana and has taught previously at the University of Toledo and the University of Michigan. He currently lives with his three younger children in Las Cruces and, when he is not writing his own books, works as a freelance writer and editor and also teaches at both New Mexico State University and Dona Ana Community College.

# Acknowledgements

I wish to thank each of the following for their invaluable contributions to the creation of this book:

Donna Eichstaedt -- Donna and I served on the Dona Ana County Historical Society Board of Directors for a number of years, including her term as President. Donna volunteered to help me with the book, and worked diligently on it. But tragically she was stricken with cancer in that time, and eventually succumbed to it. She is sorely missed.

Duncan Hayse -- Duncan came on board to fill the shoes of Donna after being recommended by the English Department of New State University. He too worked diligently on the book, but moved with his family to Texas, and that distance made it too difficult for him to continue with the project.

Evan Davies -- Evan is the founder of the Institute of Historical Survey Foundation. When he saw an early outline and slide presentation I had put together some years ago on the history of Mesilla, he strongly encouraged me to turn it into a book. The result is this book you hold today. Without his encouragement I do not think it would exist.

Cal Traylor, Bob Gamboa, Frank Parrish, and Dan Aranda were so encouraging and stimulating in many discussions of the minutia of the history of this area. They were particularly generous in offering to read a draft of the book, and to offer suggestions, comments, corrections, etc., all of which have helped to make it much better.

David Thomas -- David's outstanding deed and census research for *La Posta*, his book on Mesilla, was most helpful in compiling parts of this book, and additionally helped to prove that some of the old stories were not true. Dave shared a lot of his expertise about putting the book together and getting it published.

Rocio Velas, Denise Chavez, Cheryl Nims and my wife, Margaret Ritter -- The translation of the Albert Fountain history in this book was originally done by Rocio Vela, language specialist with the U.S. Department of Justice, and then Denise Chavez, Cheryl Nims and Margaret Ritter helped greatly in the interpretation and final drafting. The four of them are responsible for a wonderful original English version of this rarely seen document.

Jim Harris -- I had the pleasure of serving on a bank Board of Directors with Jim. When in Washington, D.C., he toured the National Portrait Gallery only to discover the oil painting "Old Mesilla Place" by Leon Trousset, circa 1885-1886. Jim, who is an outstanding photographer, sent me his photo. I am so pleased to have received permission to use it on the cover of *Mesilla Comes Alive.*

# Index

resignation as governor, 15
Rio Grande and, 55
Trenquel de la Mesilla and, 69
Organ Mountains, 68, 165
Ortiz, Ramon, 73, 74, 142
capture of, by Doniphan, 74
Otermin, Antonio de, 21
Otero, Miquel, 164
Otero County, 164
Overland Stage block, 74, 90
Oxbow lakes, 55, 56

P
Padilla, Marcial, 142
Palace of the Governors, construction of, 15
Paraje Fra Cristobal, 26
Parajes, establishment along the Camino Real, 21
Paso, 80
Picacho, 68
violence in, 120
Picacho Grant, 75
Pierce, Franklin 79, 80
Pike, Zebanon, 30
Pinkerton agents, 151
Piro Indians, 26
Plaza of La Mesilla, 143
Point of Rocks, 22
Polk, James
annexation of Mexico and, 63
attempt to buy Mexican lands, 50
cabinet meeting of, on Pacific ports, 49
signing of Gadsden Treaty, 81
Ponce de Leon, Juan, 7
Potter, Clarkson N., 147
*The Public*, 138
Pueblo Indians, 27
baptisms of, 26
structures built by, 5
take back of territory, 29
uprising of, 21
Pueblos, in Acoma, 15

Q
Quay, Matthew S., **167**

17574951R00134

Made in the USA
Middletown, DE
30 January 2015